Kids First

What Kids ~~~~~~~~~~ os
To Know About
Separation & Divorce

Authored by:

Kids First[SM] Center
Portland, Maine

TOWER
PUBLISHING

Tower Publishing, 588 Saco Road, Standish, Maine 04084-6239
www.towerpub.com

ISBN: 978-1-932056-73-0

Library of Congress Cataloging-in-Publication Data

Kids first : what kids want grown-ups to know about separation & divorce/ Kids First Center.
    p. cm.
  Summary: "A helpful guide for professionals and parents as they progress through the process of divorce. An insight into the impact their decisions will have on their children and a range of solutions available for problems which might arise"--Provided by publisher.
  Includes bibliographical references and index.
  ISBN 978-1-932056-73-0 (pbk. : alk. paper) 1. Children of divorced parents. 2. Parent and child.
  HQ777.5.K43 2008
   306.89--dc22   2008016729

Cover designed by:
Mitchell Fernie Advertising Design & Production

10 9 8 7 6 5 4

"Kids First is an honest and practical guide to providing emotional and physical well-being to children whose world is rocked by divorce. This book is preventative medicine for all divorcing parents."

~ Christiane Northrup, M.D., author of *Mother-Daughter Wisdom* (Bantam, 2005) *The Wisdom of Menopause* (Bantam revised 2006) and *Women's Bodies, Women's Wisdom* (Bantam, revised 2006)

"What Kids Want Grown-Ups to Know about Separation & Divorce is a must-read for divorced or separated parents who love their kids. As a grown-up with divorced parents, I saw my own thoughts and feelings reflected in the pages of this important guidebook. This publication is a testament to Kids First Center's core value: thoroughly kid-centric, collaborative parenting."

~ Evan Stern, Minnetonka, MN

"This book is a gold mine of information for separating parents and for the professionals who serve parents and their children. As a GAL (Guardian ad Litem), mediator and therapist who deals daily with separating parents and their children, I want to give [each parent] a copy of *What Kids Want Grown-Ups to Know About Separation & Divorce*. It will surely help lower inter-parental conflict and make life better for thousands of children affected by this issue."

~ Felicity Myers, LCSW

"Like so many parents, we were really worried about the impact of our divorce on our children. Kids First showed us that if we did things right and co-parented together, our three kids could turn out great. If you can't attend a Kids First program, this book is the next best thing."

~ Bob Stein and Susan Wuchter Stein
Divorced 1999, 3 children

"Kids First: What Kids Want Grown-Ups to Know about Separation & Divorce is the answer to a family therapist's dream. If every couple going through this difficult life stage could read this book, I feel there would be many fewer hurt children leaving a legacy of dysfunctional relationships of their own."

~ Bland Maloney, LCSW
Family Therapist

"The folks at Kids First have skillfully and caringly put the voices of children at the front of the classroom, teaching us all what it feels like to be a kid when families disrupt. This book does a superb job of translating children's expert knowledge into clear and concise language that even grown-ups can understand. I'd recommend it to parents, legal professionals, educators, and to anyone who loves a kid in a separating/divorcing family."

~Shelley Cohen Konrad, Ph.D., LCSW
Assistant Professor, University of New England

"Kids First gets it right! Parents who want their children to be well adjusted after their parents' divorce will take this information to heart and employ it consistently; especially when it is the hardest to do."

~ Susan Wiggin, LMSW, co-parent coach, Guardian ad Litem
Founder of Child-Centered Solutions

"One of the most difficult situations we have in schools is when divorced parents use the school as a battle ground. This book would help counselors and teachers and administrators understand the feelings of all parties. It also would give us some language to help the situation. This is a must read for school people and a great reference guide."

~ Mike McCarthy, Principal
King Middle School

"This book is so easy to read because it is organized and sequential. It sets the scene for the many issues that can cause problems for children as they come to understand the divorce or separation of their parents. Of particular value to the reader are the clear examples that show the cause and effect of adult behavior and children's emotions. The consistent offers of advice in each chapter on how to address issues and possible solutions leave the reader feeling empowered with a positive plan of action."

~ Tricia M.Weyand, College Placement Officer, Assembly Delegate for New England Association for College Admission Counseling
Scarborough High School

What Kids Want gives parents an honest, eye-opening perspective of divorce through a child's eyes with real-life situations from young people and adults who were children of divorce. Adults who take the time to read this book will gain useful information, insight, and resources to help the children in their lives deal with divorce."

~ Betsy Norcross Plourde, LMSW
Executive Director, Advocates for Children

"*Kids First: What Kids Want Grown-Ups to Know about Separation and Divorce* is an excellent resource for educators to understand that separation and divorce are some of the heaviest 'baggage' that students, in this situation, bring with them everyday to school. The stories told in this book give a clear picture of the impact this crisis has on kids. When you read these stories you can actually feel their pain. I feel that this book should be in every school and should be required reading for educators."

~ Vicky Johnson, Media Specialist
Richfield Springs Central School

Table of Contents

This book is dedicated to everyone who does the hard work to put kids first during the difficult times of separation and divorce.

Acknowledgements

Kids First started out in 2006 with a simple objective: to share with others the knowledge that we have gained from years of helping parents and children navigate the process of separation and divorce in a way that minimizes impact to the kids. At the start, writing a book seemed like the simplest way to do that. Now we know otherwise. This book would not have happened without the unselfish help of many, many people.

Input was provided by a great many people—facilitators of all of Kids First's programs who work routinely to support parents and children, the wonderful staff at the Center, as well as individuals who played key roles in creating and nurturing the Center. Organizing and writing the text fell to a small group—board members Al Barthelman, Terri DeCoster Grasso, Susan Livingston and Mark Tierney, as well as Executive Director Peg Libby. But knowing that "writing by committee" is not an option, Susan Livingston volunteered to spend endless hours drafting the text for the rest of us to edit – thank you, Susan, for your tireless work! And when additional pieces were needed, former board member Shelley Cohen-Konrad stepped forward to contribute, as well.

We must also acknowledge Mike Lyons and Mary Anne Hildreth, of Tower Publishing, for taking us under their wing and guiding us through a world about which we know nothing. Mike's commitment to the work that Kids First does is exemplified by his support in publishing this book.

Of course, we must acknowledge the parents and children who do the real work during and after the difficult times of separation and divorce. Kids First has evolved through supporting families during tough times and is honored to be able to share what we have learned from them by way of this book.

The thoughts and ideas that are presented in this book were contributed by the following people:

Kids First Facilitators: Betsy Van Betuw, Bob Carroll , Jim Carey, Jed French, Amy Hamilton , Michael Sandberg, Dave Webb, Patricia Weyand, Jamie Whittemore, Susan Wiggin

Kids First Staff: Krista Doherty, Peg Libby, Sheila Nee, Mary Swann

Current and Former Board Members: Cushman Anthony, Al Barthelman, Shelley Cohen Konrad, Angela Crocker, Terri DeCoster Grasso, Susan Livingston, Bob Stein, Mark Tierney

Other Supporters of Kids First: Annie Bergman, Justice A. Mark Horton, Paula Mahony, Felicity Myers, Andrew Schepard, Kirsten Skorpen, Kendall Wyman

Foreword

As a frequent visitor, I know that good things come from Maine—lobsters, memories of hiking in Acadia National Park, L. L. Bean jackets and Wild Blueberry Stonewall Kitchen jam. This book heads the list of good things from Maine for divorcing and separating parents. It is a call to parental peacemaking while families reorganize, and a concrete, practical guide on how parents can help children emerge stronger at its end.

The book is authored by Kids First Center in Portland, Maine, a unique resource that should be duplicated in every community that cares about its children. Kids First is an interdisciplinary volunteer effort of divorce lawyers, mental health professionals and the courts to give parents and children tools to turn away from conflict during family reorganization and move towards growth and healing. Kids First models the kind of cooperation between professionals, parents and children that educates and supports families in transition towards better outcomes for our most precious resource, our children.

Kids First has worked with hundreds of reorganizing families; their collective experiences are reflected in this book. I am particularly impressed by how well Kids First captures the voice of the children it has worked with in a book written for adults. As a law professor, founder of a parent education program for divorcing and separating parents, and advocate for children, I have talked with hundreds of young people caught in the middle of parental conflict that erupts when adults terminate their relationships with each other. This book beautifully states the message that they have often asked me to convey to their parents—keep us out of the middle of your conflict, let us love you both in our own way and in our own time. Actual quotations from children and parents along with true stores of hope and sadness illustrate these themes and present concrete ways parents can implement them.

A thought for divorce lawyers: read this book yourself, give it to your clients when they retain you, discuss it with them, and volunteer to work with an organization in your community like Kids First. I represented many angry and confused parents in my practice and have had intense discussions with many more in parent education sessions. Most are good people going through very difficult times. They want to do the right thing for their children, but sometimes just don't know what it is or can't control their emotional reactions. Parents look to their lawyers for guidance on how to behave in their stressful and disorienting circumstances. Kids First advises: "Parents need to measure their actions by a simple test: What do I want my kids to remember about how I behaved during the time of my separation and divorce?" Use this gift from Maine to help them answer that question in their children's best interests. You will serve as a peacemaker and a healer, one child at a time.

Andrew Schepard

Andrew Schepard is Professor of Law, Hofstra University School of Law and the Director of Hofstra University's Center for Children, Families and the Law. Professor Schepard is the editor of the *Family Court Review* and the author of *Children, Courts and Custody: Interdisciplinary Models for Divorcing Families* (Cambridge University Press 2004).

Introduction

About this book—A Guide for Professionals and Parents

In 1989, a group of legal and mental health professionals from the Portland, Maine area created the Kids First[SM] Program to help parents minimize the trauma that their separation and divorce would have on their children. This led to the creation of the Kids First Center, which opened its doors in January of 1998 and now offers a wide range of programs for children, parents and professionals who deal with the issues of separation and divorce.

This book is intended to represent the collective knowledge that has been gained by staff and volunteers at Kids First over these many years. We hope that professionals will find it to be a helpful guide as they work with families who are separating and divorcing. We also hope that parents find it a welcome insight into the impact their decisions have on their kids, the range of solutions available for every problem, and most of all the hope for a better future.

A few important points before we start:

- *Defining "family"*—From the child's point of view, the impact is the same whether their parents were married or not, whether their parents are a man and woman or of the same sex. When their parents split up, the trauma is essentially the same. The ideas in this book should apply equally to all family arrangements, with one important exception: domestic abuse situations.

- *Co-parenting versus parallel parenting*—The research is clear that children benefit in the long term by having safe, effective and ongoing parenting from both parents. It is our belief that despite the stresses of separation and divorce, most parents and children can create a new and healthy family system, one that will continue to support the children as they grow and mature. Although each parent will develop a personal style of parenting, they must demonstrate respect for their co-parent's rights and the unique relationships that they have with the children.

- *Domestic abuse: the importance of safety*—The concept of co-parenting is built on a premise that each parent will be safe when dealing with the other. In situations where there is a history or threat of physical, emotional or verbal abuse between the parents or child abuse, many of the guidelines in this book will not be applicable. Kids First offers specialized programs to support parents in a domestic abuse situation and to help professionals address this issue.

- *The challenge of representing the child's view*—In writing this book we have strived to represent the impact of separation and divorce as experienced by the child. In many instances, children speak about a divorce as "their divorce." We need to acknowledge that under any circumstance; only the children know how they actually feel. The best we can do as adults is to listen.

About Kids First—making a difference

The Kids First Center in Portland, Maine helps families through the difficult transition of separation and divorce, and provides training to professionals who want to do the same. Kids First focuses on the needs of the individual child and the individual family. Kids First is unique in its approach in several ways:

- *Multidisciplinary*—a collaborative effort by mental health and legal professionals.

- *Educational*—not therapeutic.

- *Group Oriented*—the group process imparts tools for families to improve their own individual situation.

- *Child Focused*—regularly taps into the child's perspective and communicates that insight to professionals and parents.

- *Inclusive*—serves all forms of families—traditional and non-traditional.

- *Practical*—combines knowledge from current research with practical and anecdotal data collected by Kids First professionals.

The goal of Kids First is to reduce the trauma of divorce and separation on kids. We do this by addressing the needs of everyone involved—the child, parents, legal and mental health professionals, and even judges—through a wide variety of programs.

Support groups for children include kids age 6 to 18. Children facing separation and divorce or adjusting to life after divorce come together to discuss feelings and coping skills in a safe, supportive environment. Realizing that they are not alone and sharing feelings with other kids is a large part of the healing. Leaders use discussion, creative activities, and relaxation skills as a means for kids to express themselves without fear of ramification. The *Kids Say* quotes in this book have come from children in Kids First groups. (Names have been changed to respect their privacy.)

Programs for parents have evolved to address a wide range of issues. The Center's flagship, 4-hour Kids First Program is presented by a male/female, attorney/mental health team of facilitators who impart the necessary information and tools to help smooth the separation and divorce process for everyone involved—which ultimately benefits kids. Parents get information on the effects of separation and divorce on kids of various ages and developmental stages, how to resolve conflicts, what to expect during the separation and divorce process, and how to recognize when to seek professional help.

Programs for professionals are designed to help further educate professionals within the fields of law, mental health and education who work with families going through separation and divorce. The Center's annual conference in November brings nationally-recognized experts on the subject to the State of Maine.

What Kids First knows about separation and divorce

At the Kids First Center, parents and professionals have the opportunity to read the stories and comments of actual kids who have been through the Kids First Program. These ideas are shared with other professionals to help them more fully understand the human impact of separation and divorce on families.

Separation and divorce hurts kids. Given information, education and support, this hurt can be minimized. By educating parents and professionals that <u>ongoing conflict is the number one negative impact on kids</u> and teaching new models for effective co-parenting, children can be helped through the process.

The post-separation process can be a positive experience in a new way—where the adults share a common focus of navigating the families through the minefield of conflict and discover new and different ways to love and support their children. Once separation and divorce is seen through the eyes of the child, it is clear why there has to be a Kids First way.

The Kids First[SM] Center is a recipient of the Annual Family Law Achievement Award given by the Maine Bar Association; the Agency of the Year Award given by the National Association for Social Workers, and the Community Impact Merit Award given by The Association of Junior Leagues International and the BMW Corp. Kids First programs have been listed in the Exemplary Court Programs and Practices publication put out by the Association for Family and Conciliation Courts.

More about Kids First and other helpful resources can be found at their website <u>www.kidsfirstcenter.org</u>.

Chapter One

What Separation Feels Like To Kids
(Divorce Rocks the House)

The emotional earthquake

For kids, separation and divorce can be an earthquake that rocks the house. Kids do not know when it will strike, even if some feel it coming. It is always an unsettling experience at best, and devastating at worst. The aftershocks continue to rattle the perceived stability of their lives. Separation and divorce have damaged the house; changes and repairs will be in order. Sometimes the new work is do-it-yourself, but often, professional help is required.

After separation is announced, although adults may feel relief, the scary part begins for kids. What was steadfast and sure is now teetering. The home's reassuring form is disrupted by fear and uncertainty. External intrusions from custody evaluators, judges and therapists—not to mention new partners and well-meaning relatives—descend upon the family. "Why is this happening to me?" becomes the child's refrain.

Before separation and divorce, for the kids, life was a series of predictable, recognizable routines. That is not to say that all was carefree and easy. Even chaos can become a way of life. However, the comfort of their predictable routine disappears for kids when their parents separate.

Change brings scary feelings

Separation and divorce requires the family to make many changes, such as living arrangements, finances, holidays, parenting, and family connections. Adults need to remember that change can be especially hard on children. For example,

- Have you ever woken up and not known where you are?
- Have you ever lied to protect someone else's feelings?
- Have you ever felt caught in the middle between siblings, parents or friends and not known where to turn?

Children of separation and divorce are often keenly aware of these feelings.

Changes are complicated and confusing

When parents separate and divorce, children are not simply caught in the middle. Many children speak of their parents' divorce as their own. Kids are not just bystanders; they are entangled in a complicated system of unspoken rules and expectations. Children often silently watch and listen to the adults around them, hearing more than they should. The half-truths they hear can be confusing and frightening. In an attempt to appease, children will often feed parents what they think they want to hear or even engage in overt parenting of the parents.

Twelve-year-old Brianne's parents are divorcing and her mother has a new boyfriend. Brianne shared her confused feelings like this. "I feel two-faced. When I'm with my mom, I tell her that I like her boyfriend okay. When I'm with my dad, I tell him that I hate him (the boyfriend). I guess I'm a bad person." When Brianne was asked to explore what her true feelings were, she blankly replied, "I don't know." Brianne's story demonstrates how children often feel forced to say things to parents that they do not believe or give endorsements to their parents' choices. Sadly, Brianne has concluded that she is a "liar" and therefore a "bad person."

Navigating the turmoil of separation can lead to problems for kids. Some develop maladaptive coping skills, shut down emotionally, and/or regress developmentally.

What happened to the Happy Days?

Even into adulthood, children of separation and divorce often dread what used to be the happy days. Holidays, birthdays, school plays, athletic events and vacations can become opportunities for separated parents to advance their own agendas. Kids feel even more vulnerable at these times and their memories of these events can be contaminated forever. Further, relationships within the family can be destroyed irrevocably. Family milestones and celebrations are easily overshadowed by concerns of having the two separated parents at the same event.

Parents need to measure their actions by a simple test: What do I want my kids to remember about how I behaved during the time of my separation and divorce?

Even well-meaning parents make mistakes during the high stress of holiday times. However when mistakes happen, parents can be effective role models for their kids by acknowledging the mistake, making amends and getting back on track as soon as possible.

Fallout from separation and divorce lingers long into adulthood. However, not all fallout is bad for kids. Frequently, children will express relief to have the fighting stop, to live in a calmer household.

Sometimes, separation is a relief

Lessons learned from living in a home where arguments and aggression were the norm can have serious long-term effects on a child. They may:

- Feel isolated and alone, perhaps not inviting friends to their house for fear of what they will see.
- Take personal responsibility for the safety and well-being of their parents.
- Accept violence and aggression as normal, acceptable behaviors.

Escaping that environment can be taken as a first step toward healing.

Thirty-five year old Krista remembers vividly the tensions of her parents' home. "The days were always the same: In the mornings, everyone was sullen and quiet, nursing hurt and grudges; we arrived home from school still riding the thermals of our friends and homework, control and normalcy; in the evenings, as my parents came through the door, like thunderheads, the seething rage would roll in and begin to bubble and hiss. The implied violence was everywhere—gritted teeth, slamming cupboards, crashing pans, poking fingers and grabbed arms. We learned that rage was indiscriminate and it was best to keep your head down and not make eye contact, to make yourself as small as possible so as not to draw a discharge—that acid, burning belittlement and sarcasm. Sooner or later, the storm would break. My parents would hurl their horrible words at each other and we were no longer there; they didn't see us or hear us any more.

"One night, at the table, as my parents ran down that same tired litany of arguments, screeching and barking, I felt something different accompany the usual adrenaline rush. My father had already slammed his fist down on the table and declared that he was going to get ugly and nobody was going to like it. My youngest sister, who was seven, had tears in her eyes and her face was flushed, her chest bucked as she stared down into her dinner plate. My middle sister, nine, continued to fork food into her mouth numbly but kept one wary eye on my father's fisted right hand. His pounding had sloshed her milk out of her glass and I wanted to clean it up before he noticed. Usually, I would sit there in silence, frozen, feeling hot and heavy, my stomach in a ball, the food in my mouth mealy and dry, waiting for an escape cue. Usually I was afraid, but this time the fear had turned and I was enraged. In my head it seemed endless, it was never going to stop and I was so sick of it. I couldn't watch it anymore. I couldn't LISTEN to it anymore. I stood up and I was shaking. I knew if I did this wrong, I would be annihilated—'the boom was going to come down' on my head. My parents stopped screaming. I told my sisters to go

upstairs to my room. I leaned down towards my parents in this sort of feral, quivering hunch—I couldn't stand upright and I was scaring myself—and said in a low voice that was a scream caught in my chest, that if they didn't get it together and figure it out, I was going to call my dad's sister and she would come get us and we would live with her, because I was not going to do this any more. Figure it out or we're leaving.

"We spent a day in my room, maybe more. I knew that I could save my sisters now. I could protect them. I was powerful. And I decided that my parents were gutless, moronic lunatics. They disgusted me; I would not turn to them again for anything. I closed my heart to them. I have never come back. Things have changed, things have 'gotten better' but no matter how hard I try, I still feel the same."

Parents can lessen the pain

Most parents truly want to put the interests of their kids first, but few know how to do it. In the midst of the emotional disruption of separation and divorce, making decisions in the best interest of the child can be very difficult. Even well intentioned parents can have trouble determining what those best interests are.

Good parenting is the first casualty of ongoing high conflict. The following common parental pitfalls increase the pain for kids:

- Engaging in a popularity contest between parents by spending too much money, relaxing house rules or being lax with discipline,

- Experiencing a second adolescence by partying, dating and self-indulgence,

- Treating the separation and divorce like a battle "in the name of the child," where the child is actually the loser—e.g., spending college funds on a divorce to "benefit the child,"

- Being physically present, but not emotionally available to the child due to preoccupation with the separation process, new relationships or self-discovery,

- Not being physically present for teens because they are "old enough to be on their own,"

- Extending conflict by staying in a victim role and making the other parent "pay" for breaking up the family.

Parents have a lot of influence over how painful separation and divorce is for their kids depending upon how they restructure their relationship and manage their co-parenting partnership. Unfortunately, separating and divorcing parents get less education on successful co-parenting than advice on legal maneuvering around residency and financial matters. The role of co-parenting education and well-trained professionals assisting families through separation and divorce can be as important as the parents themselves in determining a positive outcome.

Separation and divorce is not easy on anyone—kids, adults, families and friends. How kids cope and what kids need during the separation varies based on age and temperament of the child. How children remember the separation and divorce experience is largely up to the parents and their behavior.

There is one constant: kids want to love and be loved by both parents.

A child's view of separation and divorce:

- **Children often react by blaming themselves.**

- **Children often feel fear, sadness, guilt and anger.**

- **Parents and their children may have very different feelings about divorce—a parent may feel relief while the child feels sadness.**

- **Children want to know how divorce will affect them directly—Where will I live? Where will I go to school? Can I still see my friends?**

- **Children often have a fantasy of their parents reuniting.**

- **Children may feel shame and embarrassment—in the extended family and in their community.**

- **Children want to see more of the parent they are not with—and they worry about their wellbeing.**

Chapter Two

Listening to Children
(It's Important to Listen—
Though Not Always Easy)

We acknowledge that only children know how they actually feel. As adults, the best we can do is to listen. There are people who believe that adults need to make decisions for children; that kids are too young to understand what they need or how they feel. The first half of that belief is true; children shouldn't be put in the middle of complicated family decisions. Parents are the ones who need to make hard decisions in light of their children's needs. However, children are the experts on their feelings, perceptions and thoughts. Knowing a child's perspective is an important aspect (though not the only one) of post-separation/divorce decision-making.

Understanding children's feelings depends not on how the child tells the story but on how accurately the adult translates its meaning. First and foremost, adults need to have familiarity with child development. For example, young children don't have the maturity to fully comprehend divorce, but that doesn't mean they haven't figured it out for themselves.

Twelve-year-old Amanda told this story to her school counselor. When she was 6-years-old she heard her parents fighting in their bedroom. This didn't upset her because she was used to them being angry at each other. She just figured all parents fought; it was part of being grown-ups.

9

She was glad that her dad was staying home today to help her get ready for school. He let her wear whatever she liked and today she wanted to wear her new, red party shoes. Mom would have made her wear her boots because it was snowing and she wouldn't want her shiny shoes to get all wet. Moms were like that.

When Amanda got off the bus, mom scolded her for getting her shoes all wet. Amanda said that it was okay with dad; but, mom gave her a funny look. Later at dinner, mom told Amanda and her sister that dad had gone to live with Uncle Bob and wasn't going to live with them anymore. Mom said that she and dad saw things differently and they just couldn't live together any more. But Amanda knew better. She knew it was because of the shoes. For years Amanda blamed herself for the divorce.

A child's interpretation of divorce events should never be dismissed or minimized. Amanda's story may be cute to some, but it caused her undue suffering because she falsely thought she caused her family's pain and struggled to rectify the damage.

Adolescents may act seemingly unaffected by their parents' separation and deny that it bothers them at all. Everyone gets divorced; why should it bother me? This translates to: *My peers are unsympathetic, and I'll get picked on if I seem vulnerable. I can't act different than before because I'll get teased. And anyway, I have college applications and grades to worry about.*

Additionally, many teens feel that they have to take care of their parents. One or both parents may tell their teen-aged son that he's now "the man of the family." Or, teens may be given or assume increased responsibilities for taking care of the family:

Twenty-six-year old Sally says that she always felt older than all her friends. When she was 14-years-old, her parents divorced and her mother went to live in a distant state with a new boyfriend. Sally's younger siblings were devastated by their mother's relocation and her dad was overwhelmed with work and child care responsibilities.

Although he tried to be like Mom, Dad had never learned to cook, was always late getting the kids to school, and he seemed tired and grumpy. Sally babysat for Devon and Samantha all the time. It was an easy transition for her to become 'mom' to make things easier for Dad.

Sally now struggles with relationships of her own. Although she believes she gained maturity and didn't fall into the typical adolescent pitfalls like some of her friends, she also resents missing out on a big chunk of her childhood playing 'Sister Mom.' She wishes that her parents had realized she was just a kid and that it was their job, not hers, to be parents. But she never brings it up with them because they're all happier now and after all, didn't it all work out for the best?

Listening to teens can be difficult. It is hard not to take their attitudes and words personally. But it's important for parents to take Sally's advice and remind themselves that despite their deepening voices, changing bodies and needs for appropriate separation, adolescents are still kids. Some parents say that talking in the car helps because you don't need to make eye contact. Counselors can be helpful because despite all the myths, adolescents appreciate being listened to and cared about. Children of any age want their views to be heard and considered.

How to listen for what is not said

Many adults might ask why Amanda and Sally had not simply told their parents what and how they were feeling. Certainly it would make life easier if we could all be clear about our thoughts and comfortable with sharing our honest feelings. But it only takes a moment of self reflection to admit that sharing our feelings, even with those we love, is never a simple matter.

First and foremost, adults need to stand in children's shoes if they are going to be able to hear their voices. There are many obstacles for children to authentically share their feelings with adults and many roadblocks to parents' complete understanding:

- Listening needs to occur through a developmental lens. Learn about child development.

- Children are taught to respect adult authority and decision-making. When children's feelings challenge adults' decisions or make grown-ups angry, children will keep their feelings to themselves.

- Adults have the power to punish or take things away. Children feel if they challenge or behave in ways that make waves, they could lose privileges or, even worse, they could lose love.

- Children do not respond well to direct questioning. They will likely say what you want to hear or say nothing at all. Parents should take advantage of a moment of closeness or create opportunities for uninterrupted time for conversations to unfold.

- Children may tell you a lot without words. Children tend to show distress, confusion or ambivalence through behaviors. Be observant and notice themes or patterns in your child's behaviors.

- Don't assume. Children understand the world differently from adults. Here are some examples:

Lenny, a 4-years-old, wanted to go to heaven. He couldn't understand why his mother was acting so scared and why she was taking him to a counselor. He loved the way heaven looked so nice and quiet in his children's Bible. He thought it was funny when the counselor asked why he wanted to die. Lenny didn't want to die, he just wanted to visit heaven when the fighting in his house got too bad. He was surprised when the counselor told him that once you go to heaven you don't get to come back. Lenny was disappointed that he couldn't go to heaven but he could at least think about it in his mind when he wanted to get away.

Cara's parents were really surprised when she became anxious and depressed upon learning of her father's impending marriage. The seven-year-old had adapted so well to their split and they had done everything to make the transitions easy for her and her 10-year-old brother, Ethan. They spent all holidays together, birthdays were shared and they never, ever fought in front of the kids. What came to light was that Cara had heard the words divorce at age three but had not really understood what it meant. She thought divorce just meant living in different houses (which is what she was told). What she saw was her parents being happy together. What she experienced was positive family time with mom, dad, and Ethan. It was only now that dad was getting married that the real meaning of divorce was taking hold, and Cara was very, very sad.

- Be genuinely curious, ask questions and listen respectfully and don't dismiss the child's version of the story.

Hearing the child as expert

As noted above, the ability to understand divorce from the child's perspective relies less on the child's ability to convey his/her feelings but on the quality of parents' capacities to listen effectively. Studies with children tell us that the better understood children feel, the more likely they will successfully adapt to the challenges of divorce. To understand children's perspectives, adults (including parents, lawyers, mental health practitioners, and judges) need to view children as experts in their experiences. This requires that adults convey a sense of value in what children have to say. Inviting children to participate in the larger conversation about divorce makes them feel included as valid members of the family. However, it is important as well to let them know that the adults will make the final decisions. Knowing that their parents are still in charge assures children that are still being cared for. When children feel included and heard within the safety net of parental structure and love they are better able to handle the bumpy road ahead and thrive.

Listening requires tolerating difficult emotions

No parent wants their child to suffer. Parents will do whatever they think best to protect their children from distress or sorrow. However, it is critical for parents to understand that children are inevitably hurt and suffer a loss when divorce occurs. Parents need to prepare themselves to be discomforted and anticipate the expected and normal distress that divorce brings about for children. Children need to express their fears, anger and sorrow to the adults with whom they feel safe. The inability to tolerate a child's pain is a significant obstacle to listening. It also leads to poor decision-making and to mishandling aspects of the separation and divorce.

There is no simple strategy for tolerating our children's pain and distress. But the following represent ways to get around common pitfalls.

- Don't avoid talking to your child about their difficult feelings. Mentioning sadness does not cause sadness. Children feel relieved when you name what they are feeling.

- Don't assume that children are happy because their parents are happy.

- Don't discredit children's feelings. Although most children do 'get over it,' they don't like to hear parents or other adults belittle what they are feeling in the moment.

- Just listen. Don't fix. And don't make promises you can't keep.

Twenty-nine-year-old Alex recalls how his mother fell all over herself to make things better for him and his two brothers when his parents were separating. Dad moved out and set up a household with Liz, his now stepmother, right after the kids were told. Alex knew that didn't bode well for their future relationship. But Mom kept reassuring him of his dad's love and devotion, and promised that once the divorce was over Dad would be able to be a better father. It didn't happen. And although 18 years later Alex understood his mother's intentions, he still resented that neither parent honestly prepared him for the hurt and pain of the divorce.

- Prepare yourself that your child will be angry at you. Listen to what he or she has to say without immediately blaming the other parent.
- Believe in the power of relationships to heal. Staying connected to your children's feelings, hearing their pain and valuing their expertise will help them make a positive transition to post-divorce life.

Listening, learning and the children's best interests

Listening helps parents to more accurately understand their children's experiences of divorce. When parents can share with each other what they have learned by listening, filter it through knowledge of child development, and apply it knowing their children's personalities and temperaments, they are better equipped to make decisions that will support their children's best interests.

Even judges find it difficult to listen to children's suffering. One judge wrote that divorce decisions are really difficult even when both parents are good caretakers. Knowing that children are going to be hurt, and recognizing that any decision short of bringing parents back together will cause necessary suffering makes even judges feel helpless. Another judge wrote, "Usually when I am forced to make a decision, everyone is unhappy."

Listening to children and valuing their expertise not only helps children but it helps adults make more accurate decisions that will be durable over time.

Chapter Three

Telling Kids about the Separation
(*The Day Time Stands Still*)

Parents have only one opportunity to make a first good impression

No matter how much time passes, most kids remember every detail of when their parents told them about the separation. Sights, sounds, weather and time all adhere to young memories.

Twenty-five year old Kristin remembers back twenty years ago when, on a hot summer night, her uncle came to visit. Kristin and her brother had picked summer squash from the garden that day. They had looked forward to the squash for dinner, but that evening they were fed separately and put to bed early. They were confused and disappointed not to enjoy the fruits of their labor.

A little while later, Kristin's mom came to the kids' bedroom and shared a bowl of hot, steamed summer squash with Kristin and her brother. Kristin was surprised her mom would bring the food to her bedroom after she was already in bed.

"I was even more surprised when I realized Mom really came to tell me that my father had left with my uncle and that he would not be living with us at our house anymore. She was very sad, which made me very sad.

19

My two year old brother did not understand what was happening. As a result, he was the only one who enjoyed the summer squash. I will never forget the night my dad moved out and my parents became separated."

Difficulties are inherent for parents and kids

Telling the kids about separation is tough, especially when parents are focused on their own misery. Regardless of good intentions, the dreaded moment is filled with emotions about the other partner as much as its effect on the kids. When talking with kids about the separation, one of the most difficult tasks for parents is managing their own feelings and fears.

Parents may have perceptions about their children that have less to do with the children and more to do with the way the parents are dealing with the separation. For example, the parent who wants the divorce often views the children as adjusting well, whereas the parent who does not want the divorce views the children as very distressed and not adjusting at all.

When nine-year-old Robert's father told him that he and his mother were getting divorced, Robert believed he was going to an orphanage. He held this fear for two years and never told a soul until he participated in a children's support group at age eleven.

The kids are not prepared for what is coming when they receive the announcement of the separation. They are ill-equipped to recognize and understand their feelings, much less express and manage them. In addition, kids want to stay where life was familiar. They may fear losing a parent; they may think they can do something to make the separation go away. Usually, kids want to turn back the clock. On the other hand, by the time most parents tell their kids about divorce, the adults have been thinking for a long time about getting on with a life separate from their co-parent.

Kids frequently take cues from their parents during uncertain times. Parents need to provide positive, consistent messages which take the kids' feelings into account.

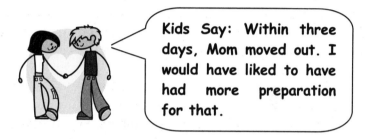

Kids Say: Within three days, Mom moved out. I would have liked to have had more preparation for that.

Younger children especially have difficulty grasping the meaning of events that will happen sometime in the future. "Are we there yet?" is a repeated question on a road trip. Future changes resulting from their parents' separation are even more confusing.

Parents help kids by taking time to be well-prepared

The biggest problem occurring during early parental negotiations about separation and divorce is a failure to objectively focus on the well-being of the kids. Each separating parent needs some time to deal with his or her own fear, hurt and anger in order to put a perspective on what is going to happen in the future. Time can help parents gain some control over their lives and may tame volatile or unruly emotions. This is especially important when one partner originates the separation and the other partner is not in agreement.

Planning for how to tell the kids about separation may take a long time due to anger and disagreement. If conversations become unproductive, parents may find it helpful to resume discussions at a later, agreed-upon time. In addition, parents may need time for professional assistance if either parent feels it would be helpful or if either parent feels the other is obstructing a positive announcement.

Kids Say: My brother and I were very angry, and we were not sure what we were angry about.

Well-prepared parents can plan their responses to hard questions kids are likely to ask, such as:

- Where will I live and who will take care of me?

- Where will each parent live?

- When will I see each parent?

- Where will the pets live?

- What will happen with sports and activities?

- Who else knows?

- Is another person involved?

- Will I stay at the same school?

- What will happen at birthdays and holidays?

- Do you still love each other?

- Is this temporary?

Guidelines for telling the kids

All families are different. However, some general guidelines apply. In addition to the preparation suggested above, parents should consider the following:

- Be together and be united in the discussion, if at all possible.

- Do not blame the other parent.

- Provide a consistent message.

- Reassure kids they are loved and safe.

- Focus on the future.

- Tell kids what is certain. Do not make up what is not certain. Do not give false security. Do not give information unless it is agreed upon by both parents.

- Introduce change as slowly as reasonably possible.

- Limit the personal details. No matter how old the kids, there is no benefit to discussing all the details that led to the divorce. Some details never need to be told.

Kids Say: I want to know only the vague reasons for the divorce, not all the details.

- Keep it simple. Kids are not able to understand many adult issues of separation and divorce.

- Gear the initial discussion toward the younger children; let all kids know both parents are available for future, individual discussions.

- Avoid holidays, birthdays and other significant dates for this painful discussion.

- Avoid telling kids that everything is better this way.

- Provide kids with ideas about grown-ups who are available for support, such as family members, teachers, clergy, professional counselors or professionals at the Kids First Center or similar programs.

- Reassure kids they are not the cause; the separation is not their fault; and, they cannot fix it.

- Give them permission to express how they feel about the separation and divorce, even if it is negative.

Parents minimize the kids' confusion when their first priority is to present a united front, showing respect for the other parent. Consistency is a universal maxim of good parenting. It is especially necessary during the tender days of separation.

Jason, age twelve, was comforted when his dad assured him, "Don't you worry. You'll be able to stay in your home for as long as you want." Jason had lived there since his birth and it was just down the street from his middle school.

Unfortunately, Jason's parents did not value the importance of presenting a consistent message to the kids. Dad assumed Mom would stay in the home. She had requested it in the divorce so, of course, she would stay there. Dad thought he was being helpful by giving Jason assurances about his residence.

When Jason came home from school one day, he saw a 'for sale' sign on his front lawn. Jason experienced two losses: the loss of his home and the loss of confidence in his dad's word.

Kids Say: Be sure to tell kids that it's not their fault. We kids don't really believe that, but it helps to hear it anyway.

Kids' needs after hearing the news

As stated in the guidelines above, the first discussion about divorce involves both parents and all the children. Thereafter, it is helpful for parents, individually or together, to speak with each child separately and discuss the divorce at a level each will understand. Care and coordination in planning when and where to do this will aid in a constructive discussion.

Children of different ages and temperaments will want varying information and security. A parent who is empathetic and well-informed about putting kids first is in the best position to determine what to say and how to listen to each child.

Once the news of separation or divorce occurs, parents should watch to see how their kids are doing. However, two general problems may interfere:

- Kids' responses are unclear. Many children are not inclined to talk about their feelings or do not have the words to express themselves. They may need help identifying what they are feeling. They need reassurance that all their feelings are real and valid.

- Parents' observations are subjective. When parents separate, their focus naturally shifts onto their individual relationship with the kids. When uncertainty exists about the new residential arrangement, parents may be protective and reluctant to discuss kids' feelings honestly.

In order to obtain a more objective view of their kids' well-being, parents should enlist the assistance of teachers, daycare providers or other trustworthy individuals who have regular contact with the kids. In addition, kids may find comfort knowing there are some supportive adults, including but not limited to professionals, with whom they can speak openly. A kids' support group, such as the one at the Kids First Center or similar programs, helps kids see they are not alone.

Kids may also need their parents to obtain some professional resources. When battling parents agree to work out their differences with the assistance of a co-parenting counselor or mediator, the kids are the beneficiaries of those extra efforts.

Kids Say: The experience, being caught in the middle like that, erased all my memories of what happened before, so that I have no real memories of any good times.

Kids need parents to monitor their responses to the separation on an ongoing basis. Not all reactions come quickly. Telling the kids about the separation is the beginning step of a long process. When the move occurs, it triggers more life disruptions. Kids may take years to achieve a comfortable state of stability. Kids need parents to hang in there with them.

Some warning signals

Kids' behavior may be a signal to their parents to obtain professional advice. Symptoms such as the following, when they are beyond the normal range for that individual child, may serve as indicators.

- Developmental regression
- Changes in sleep patterns or eating habits
- Frequent nightmares
- Extreme sadness/despair
- Extreme responsibility or obedience
- Behavior problems at school
- Isolation
- Explosive anger or rages
- Intense, unrealistic fears
- Violent behavior toward self or others

These behaviors are not necessarily the fault of the other parent; although, it is not unusual for them to occur only in one household. Parents can work together to help children overcome problematic behaviors regardless of where they are expressed.

Most children have an acute sensitivity to the nature of their parents' relationship. When they feel the ongoing tension that comes from conflict and arguments, there may be serious long-term effects. The children may:

- Feel a sense of responsibility for the abuse
- Take on a parental role toward one or both parents
- Exhibit more aggressive behavior
- Generate attitudes that justify use of violence

- Isolate themselves out of shame

When separating, cooperating with the co-parent is the most basic and most important step parents can take to minimize their kids' pain—assuming of course that it is safe. All the factors that go into general good parenting take on greater importance during separation and divorce.

Chapter Four

Steps Toward a
Healthy Co-Parenting Partnership
(The Relationship Goes On)

Developing a meaningful life and support team

During the first stages of separation, people often report feeling like an adolescent again—not surprisingly, for adolescence is a time of figuring out who one is. Separated parents do well to begin the process of re-establishing their sense of self-worth and identity as soon as possible. The time of reappraisal can offer an opportunity to pursue aspects of life previously unexplored or unavailable.

Mike and Nora functioned as a family unit with strong divisions of responsibility. Mike was the breadwinner and handled all of the bills for the family. Nora kept the home and arranged family activities. She had never balanced a checkbook. The family was heavily in debt and money issues were a constant source of battles. Mike blamed Nora for overspending; Nora blamed Mike for not providing for the three kids. They had no idea how they would be able to run two households when history showed there was not enough money to run one.

A year later, Nora ran into her attorney in the grocery store. "You have no idea how good my life is," stated Nora. "I discovered that when I was in charge of my own finances, I was really good at budgeting. It became a game for me to minimize my expenditures without sacrificing the quality of my life. The kids and I live in a small home that we renovated ourselves. We have a great time there. I am no longer angry at Mike because my life is so much better now."

When parents are able to develop a new meaningful life of their own, their kids are relieved of the burden of worrying about their parents' well-being. Kids have a big job to get themselves through the split up of their family. A visibly needy or distraught parent adds an additional burden to the kids.

Kids do not need parents to always put on a happy, "Pollyanna" face. Down times are part of loving and being human. When parents demonstrate appropriate sadness they provide a model for expressing emotions. If, in addition to expressing sadness, parents also address their new life issues in a productive and healthy manner, their kids will be in a better position to move forward in their own lives.

A support team of friends, community groups and professionals (mental health, physical health, legal and financial) greatly enhances a person's ability to adapt to the many changes of the separation and divorce process. Friends and family members who are positive and constructive are a valuable separation resource. On the other hand, parents are wise to beware of the well-intentioned family member or friend who fuels the fire. A little bit of grousing may clear the mind somewhat, but anyone who encourages anger and focuses on past acts may derail the hard work of problem solving for a successful future.

Community groups may be found by checking local newspapers, public radio stations and local access television channels. Some groups focus on individual transition and development. Others, like the Kids First Center or similar programs, help parents understand how they and their children are affected by the separation. Most community groups focusing on parental separation can recommend professionals who may be helpful to parents and children.

Achieving a balance between parents' and kids' needs is a matter of trial and error. The fact that circumstances are changing very quickly during the separation and divorce process makes the balancing even more difficult. A strong and appropriate support system can help parents gain control over their own lives so that they are available to hear and see their kids' problems and needs.

Kids Say: No nasty comments in front of the kids.

Supporting the other parent

Ten year old Johnny wished his parents supported each other. One day he stood on a pitcher's mound. One out to go and Johnny's team would be town champs. On the sidelines was the usual assortment of fans, mostly parents, including Johnny's. Divorced, one stood on the first base side and the other near third base.

When Johnny retired the final batter, parents ran on to the field to share in their kids' celebration. But Johnny's parents did not move. Unable to put their differences aside for even a few minutes, they refused to be on that field together.

Because Johnny's parents stood frozen on the sidelines, Johnny stood frozen on the mound, not knowing where to turn. What should have been one of the greatest moments in his life had turned into one of the worst.

This story is played out every day. Not always on a ball field and not always in plain view of others, but it is a scene many kids know too well.

Ideas for a co-parenting partnership

The relationship between parents is not over at the time of separation; it is just different. Parenting is forever. Communication has to continue. The best results will occur when the parents reframe their relationship into a co-parenting partnership as follows.

- They assume characteristics of courteousness, respectfulness and a relatively formal, low-key approach.

- They are careful with language, both verbal and non-verbal. For example, rolling one's eyes can say more than a verbal slur.

- They say positive things to the child about the other parent. This reinforces that it is OK for the child to love each parent.

- They maintain a positive attitude when listening to their kids talking about the other parent.

- They allow reasonable access to the other parent even when it is not that parent's time for contact. For example, a phone call to Dad while at Mom's house.

- They do not make plans or interfere when it is the other parent's time with the children.

- They make regular appointments, by phone, by e-mail, or in person, to discuss children's issues and needs. They agree to resume the discussion later if one or the other becomes angry. If necessary, they may find email to be a less threatening approach. And, that gives them a written summary of agreements to plans.

- They do not expect appreciation, praise or emotional support from the other parent.

- They accept that each parent has authority and responsibility for day-to-day care when the kids are with that parent. One no longer has the right to judge the other parent's adequacy, beyond basic safety issues, or to insist on certain behaviors that meet one's own standards.

- They respect each other's privacy by not asking personal questions and by not grilling the kids about the other parent's life.

- They do not dredge up old transgressions.

- They do not stop communicating. Non-communication is a form of fighting.

- They let the children know that they communicate regularly, so the children can see they can put aside their differences and plan co-operatively for them.

A simple gesture can ease a lot of pain

Parents have the ability to bring great joy to their kids just by making a simple gesture of goodwill toward the other parent, even if forced.

Corey was a sixth grader comparing experiences about separation and divorce with other kids his age. The group had lots of stories about the complicated logistics of two households and the pain of separation. When the kids were asked what made them most happy, Corey's face lit up and he reported to the group: "What makes me the happiest is when my Mom and Dad laugh together."

Corey's response speaks volumes about what really matters to kids. Faking a smile to the other parent might be the best gift a kid could receive.

Understanding kids' feelings and reactions to parental separation

All children are unique individuals. No one can accurately state how all children will behave or feel. At Kids First we have observed, however, that many children do respond to their parents' separation in similar ways.

Kids Say: It's OK to like one parent more for a while. We still love you both. It can change over time.

Being open and honest

Many parents simply are not aware of the pain kids feel when one parent's personal struggle with the other is aired in front of the child. Honesty does not mean full disclosure. There are many things adults appropriately keep from children, and that is no different during separation and divorce.

Dora came to Kids First believing she was the parent who had done all the work. She bristled at the concept of being a co-parenting partner when the other parent had a history of broken promises about payment, appearances at appointments, timeliness and honesty.

"I am the Mom who calls school to make sure she gets on the right bus, packs an emergency change of clothes, who is 10 minutes early for every meeting, who thinks of all the little things the other forgets.

"My partner, on the other hand, is the type who lives on a whim, is often late, pays most bills with the 10 day grace period, if at all, forgets important details and stresses over nothing. I wanted to be recognized for my hard work and I wanted him to be punished for his lack of concern."

The Kids First class was difficult and uncomfortable for Dora. However, she came to see what it meant to take the high road and put kids first.

"The truth is...NONE of that matters to my daughter. She worships the ground her father walks on. She loves us both equally and we had to learn that for ourselves. Our child did not care how we felt about payments, appointments, etc. <u>She simply wanted to be able to love us both without feeling like she was betraying the other</u>.

"Kids First reminded us that our feelings should not play a part in our parenting skills. Story time does not change because of what Daddy did to upset Mommy last week. Children should feel comfortable saying, "I rode in Daddy's new car yesterday," without fearing Mommy getting angry because he owes her money. Our daughter has no reason to know details of our problems or financial status."

Kids Say: Do not influence the kids to dislike the other parent.

Dealing with an uncooperative or drop-out parent

- **Ideas for helping kids when there is an uncooperative parent**

Ideally, both parents can support a healthy co-parenting arrangement. However, just as it only takes one person to decide on divorce, it only takes one parent to eliminate the possibility of co-parenting. In some cases, the best course of action may simply be acceptance of the fact that the other parent is not going to change. The parent interested in co-parenting may have to accept that the other household is beyond their reach. There may be nothing to be done about bedtime, food choices, manners, discipline, etc. when the uncooperative parent is in charge.

Sometimes, when a parent accepts that the other parent is not going to be an effective co-parent the result is reduced frustration. Using Dora's words:

"Am I still the Mom who feels like I do all the work? Yes, I am. Does it make a difference to my child? No! I realized my partner was not going to change his habits because we got divorced. I will always be the over-achieving mother."

Conflict and discord between the parents can create divided loyalties in the kids. As a result, some kids may filter what they tell each parent to support the other parent's position. Kids also may hide what they like about the other parent or the other household in order to avoid conflict. Co-parenting is the best way to eliminate these sad, stressful attempts of a child to protect an angry parent. However, if co-parenting is impossible, at least one parent can rise above the fray, build trust and cut the child's discomfort in half.

Kids Say: Don't take the kid without the other parent knowing. Don't take things from the house without permission.

- **Ideas for helping kids when one parent is mostly absent**

One attentive, loving parent can be sufficient for kids to thrive in circumstances where the other parent is mostly absent from the kids' lives.

Even though Robert's dad stopped coming, calling and writing, Robert's mom never said a bad word about him. They still visited his grandmother (his father's mom) and his aunt occasionally. Robert missed his dad and wondered where he was and what he was doing. By not bad-mouthing his father, his mother left the "door open" just in case he decided to contact them, which he did shortly before his dad died. It did give Robert and his brother some feeling of resolution.

While negative comments about the other parent are only hurtful, some positive steps include:

- *You can count on me:* If one parent drops out of the children's lives, the remaining parent can build trust by assuring the children that they have a parent they can count on, rather than highlighting the absence of the other parent. A positive, trustworthy attitude can help the child develop realistic ways of coping.

- *You are lovable:* The steadfast parent can build kids' self-esteem by letting them know how lovable they are. That way kids understand that the other parent's absence is not a reflection on them.

Kids Say: It's never good to know how angry one parent is at the other. That just hurts.

Chapter Five

Kids' Residence
(Taking the High Road)

Where will the kids live?

Residential changes and schedules that come with separation are always difficult.

Bart and Julia were planning a separation while son Justin was getting ready to go into his senior year of high school. Justin was distraught about the possibility of having to leave his home during what he considered to be the most important year in his life. In response to his pleas, the parents promised Justin he would be able to stay in his own house for senior year.

Bart and Julia could barely afford to keep the house when they were all together, but they had made a promise to Justin and searched for a way to keep their promise. They had heard about the residential arrangement called nesting whereby the kids stay in the family home and the parents move in and out for their residential stays. Together, Bart and Julia rented a small, inexpensive apartment in the same town so that each of them could live in it while the other parent was residing with Justin in the family home. They alternated weeks, moving back and forth from the family home to the apartment.

By the time of graduation, Bart reported, "It just about killed us. I was so stressed out. I was having stomach pains; I had a really hard time at work; my concentration level was zilch. I felt like a bagboy; I was constantly trying to keep track of papers, books, calendars, personal belongings. It was a nightmare."

Bart now thinks all separating parents should be court ordered to spend some time going back and forth between two households and letting the kids stay put. "Just one month would do it," he says, "and then they would have some appreciation of what kids have to go through. This year 'about killed' us, but now we realize it could have 'about killed' Justin instead."

Making the arrangements in the kids' best interest is tough, especially when emotions are exploding, there is not enough money and parents are working hard just to keep their own lives together. The first step can be to find the right words to avoid making matters worse.

The language of separation and divorce

"Nesting" is a nurturing word, but may be a practical nightmare for most parents. Other phrases and words about separation may inadvertently be conveying negative feelings, for the parents and the kids. Phrases and words such as "broken home" and "visitation" can interfere with a positive perception of the new residential arrangement. Some suggestions for helping kids feel less marginalized include:

- The marriage *ended*, instead of the marriage *failed*.

- *Parenting arrangements* instead of *custody* and *visitation*.

- *Contact with* or *time with* instead of *lives with* and *visits*.

States use many different terms in their laws governing parental rights and responsibilities. Issues such as decision making, residence, custody, contact, and child support are identified by key words which may vary in meaning from state to state. Parents who educate themselves about the meanings of such terms will be in a better position to navigate the legal system.

Some common residential arrangements

If handled properly, a wide variety of residential arrangements can be healthy for kids. When parents are able to put their own interests on the sideline, they can concentrate on the kids' well-being and engage in some practical problem solving.

The range of options available for parenting is often limited by the circumstances of the parents' own lives. For example, parents living close together have more options than parents living far apart. Once a residential option is selected and implemented, it may need to be fine-tuned or even overhauled as kids get older and circumstances change. Some common arrangements include the following:

- **Sharing two homes**

This pattern assumes the kids live in two homes for approximately equal periods of time. Some common arrangements are schedules where the kids:

o Alternate their residence weekly so that kids live one week in Dad's home and one week in Mom's,

o Divide the week with half in each household, or

o Spend the school year in one home and most holidays, vacations and summers in the other home, when distance is a factor.

▲ Positives for Kids: Significant relationships with both parents are assured, for the most part. This can be good for the self-esteem of parents and children.

▼ Negatives for Kids: Frequent switches can be hard for kids unless they are handled very thoughtfully and with a high degree of cooperation. Transitions can cause serious problems when there is conflict and anger between parents. Teens often have difficulty with alternating patterns if they prevent consistent accessibility to peers, school and activities.

- **Primary residence in one home with significant, ongoing contact with other parent**

In this arrangement, children have one home base with frequent contact with the other parent each weekend and/or during the week. Major time during the summer and holidays may be scheduled.

▲ Positives for Kids: Kids may feel more stability having a primary home. Kids can have significant relationships with both parents.

▼ Negatives for Kids: Again, transitions may be difficult if there are frequent exchanges between parents. Kids may perceive they have one parent for their work life and one for their play life.

- **One residence with limited contact with the other parent**

    Kids see the other parent every other weekend and a few weeks or a month in the summer.

    ▲ Positives for Kids: Very stable and clear home base from which to operate. It may be necessary when there is high conflict between parents.

    ▼ Negatives for Kids: May inhibit the relationship with the parent who has limited contact. The residential contact parent may become overburdened and may be less available to the kids.

- **No contact or only supervised contact with one parent**

    This may occur when one parent has abandoned the kids, when there is documented abuse of children or other serious problems, such as severe mental illness or substance abuse.

    ▲ Positives for Kids: Physical safety is safeguarded and exposure to abusive or threatening situations is avoided. One stable home can provide the solid, emotional base needed by these children.

    ▼ Negatives for Kids: Kids may idealize the absent parent and may struggle more with identity issues when one parent is absent. They may experience feelings of abandonment.

Kids Say: Allow some input from us when you make decisions.

Determining the best residential arrangement

• **Guidelines by kids' ages**

The age and development of the children should be considered when making residential arrangements. Additionally, as kids develop, their needs change and the parenting arrangement may need to change with the needs of the kids. Parents who study developmental tasks and separation and divorce risks will be better prepared to make a plan that fits their child's age and developmental needs. Some basic needs at different ages include:

- **Infants and Toddlers** require strong emotional attachments to important caretaker(s) and trust in their surroundings. Attachment to both parents after separation can be promoted by frequent contacts and by providing real parenting opportunities for both parents.

- **Two and a half to five years** require security around basic needs being met—food, shelter, parental contact, consistent transition logistics. Feelings of abandonment may result in sadness and/or interfere with development.

- **Six to eight years** require developing peer and community relationships. Self-concept is developing around competence. Fears of losing a parent or fears related to basic needs, such as food and a place to live may interfere with school achievement or may result in acting out.

- **Nine to twelve years** require developing proficiency in academics, sports, arts and social settings. They are aware of their vulnerability and may feel lonely or follow negative role models.

- **Thirteen to eighteen years** require preparing for psychological emancipation and handling sexual feelings. They place peer needs ahead of family, which may complicate a residential schedule.

- ## Guidelines when parents differ

Caring parents of pure heart and generous spirit may differ as to what is in the best interest of their kids when it comes to deciding on a residential arrangement. Caring parents of broken heart and wounded spirit are even more likely to differ. Some suggestions to find the proper balance between differing perceptions are:

- **Ask "Who will really benefit from what I am proposing?"** It is difficult to separate personal feelings from parenting agendas. A parent may need assistance from others (professional counselors or objective, wise friends) to look into the future and answer this question.

- **Ask for input from the kids.** Kids should not feel that they have the burden of choosing one parent or another. However, depending on their age, they may want to make some suggestions about their schedule. If such suggestions can be incorporated into the schedule, kids can feel some control over their lives. Many kids complain that they are forced into a pattern designed only for their parents' convenience. Parents might ask what schedule would work best for the kids, in very general terms, being clear that the final decision is theirs.

  Other kids may not be able to articulate their suggestions, or they may not want to. Parents can still obtain their kids' input by carefully watching their behavior and adjustment.

- **Ask the crystal ball.** How will kids look at their post-separation childhood when they are adults? By looking down the road twenty years, a parent can gain a perspective on the decisions they are making today.

- **Listen to the other parent.** Upset or wounded parents sometimes avoid an opinion from the one other person in the world who loves the kids most. Truly listening to the other parent, in a way that thinks through what is being said, supplies insight into the big picture of what is in the kids' best interest. The listening may not lead to agreement, but at a minimum, it presents information to ponder.

- **Listen to professionals.** Parents can try out their ideas on a therapist or mediator and ask if they are truly focusing on the kids' needs or on their own.

- **Consider the schools.** The school community is an important consideration in residency. Once a decision is made, schools should be informed.

> Kids Say: We don't want to know details. We don't want to hear criticism. We don't want to provide therapy.

Managing disputes

When parents battle about residential schedules, the disputes between parents frequently hurt the kids more than a bad schedule.

Twenty-three year old Christine remembers with horror and stomach pains the Thanksgivings she spent as a child. Beginning at noon, the crowd would gather at her mother's home with her stepfather, his kids and lots of family members. She recalled, "We kids didn't care about eating turkey; all we wanted to do was play together! But as soon as things were just getting good, like all the Barbie clothes were spread out on the floor, we had to go sit down and eat the dreaded turkey, using good manners and proper grammar."

The whole family had to eat early so that Christine could be delivered to her father's Thanksgiving. "I would fight back tears in the car, even when I was a teenager. It wasn't that I didn't want to see my father. I just didn't want to leave. I knew the other kids were free to go to the playroom and have fun."

By late-afternoon, Christine was over at her father's Thanksgiving. Everyone there had been waiting for her arrival before sitting down to dinner. "I had to go through the hugging of all the old relatives and then we immediately went to the table for another turkey and more polite behavior. The kids there had been playing all day before dinner and it was hard to break into their games and jokes. I would cry myself to sleep. My father would wonder what he had done wrong. I didn't want to hurt his feelings and tell him I just wanted to stay in one place."

Christine's mother and father had both provided their daughter with what they saw as wonderful family Thanksgiving celebrations. They both loved their daughter dearly and wanted her included in their family gatherings. In their attempt to keep their daughter near to them, they just did not stop to think about what Christine's day was like.

Some kids report they like having two Thanksgivings. All kids are different; all family circumstances vary. Christine's story illustrates <u>it is not a feather-in-the-parental-cap to fight to gain equal or more time with their kids</u>. Sometimes doing what is best for the kids means letting go of the conflict and trusting there is enough love to go around for everyone, even if it means losing some time on the actual holiday.

When parents do not agree on a residential schedule, they put the decision in the hands of a judge who is essentially a complete stranger. All children are unique and no one knows them better than their parents. It is better to employ some problem solving and practicality between the parents.

Judge Smith reports he has a standard lecture he gives to parents who have requested a trial after not being able to determine the best interest of their children. In his lecture he says "I am gravely concerned about two parents who would give up their parental decision-making regarding the biggest issues in children's lives and who would hand that power over to a person in a black robe who has never met the children, will never meet the children and knows very little about them. How can a judge who does not know these children make a better decision for children than their own parents?"

Tips for negotiating a residential arrangement

- Work out as many specifics in advance as possible and write them down. Try to foresee a variety of possibilities.

- Be as specific as possible in the written document. Parents who are in agreement can always change a detail of a contact/residential schedule if they both want to deviate. However, in the event of a disagreement, the written document provides a resolution.

- Consider how the needs and wants of the kids will change over time as they mature and change schools/friends/interests.

- Consider the kids' reactions to the schedule, without looking for ammunition to use against the other parent.

- Think out of the box: <u>There is always another solution to the situation</u>. Creative parents do not let mistakes or missteps stand in the way of continuing the quest for a residential arrangement that meets everyone's needs.

Chapter Six

Kids' Transitions
(*Kids Caught in the Revolving Door*)

Walking on hot coals

"Hurry up, hurry up, hurry up!" How many times do parents say that to kids over the course of their childhoods? Transitions are notoriously difficult for kids. Just getting out the door in the morning for school or day camp can be a monumental task, requiring organization and patience.

When the child of separated parents transitions from one parent to the other, the frenzy intensifies. In addition to the hard job of physically making the move, many children fear there will be conflict, tension or arguing during the transition time. One of these kids reported, "It's like walking over hot coals to move from one parent to the other."

After the hot coals are walked on, different environments, different rules and different expectations greet the young travelers. What they do and 'how it all works' changes. Kids complain they are not given a transition time.

Kids Say: As soon as you get to the other parent's house, that parent is so excited to see you there is no down time, no time to put your things away and you are, all of a sudden, expected to be right back in the groove of things.

Supporting the other parent helps kids during transition

Parents support their kids' transitions to the other parent when they let them know:

- It's OK to have fun and enjoy time at the other parent's home.

- It's OK to look forward to seeing the other parent at transition time.

- It's OK to feel sad about leaving one parent behind and missing what is at that house.

Ten-year-old Charley has been transitioning between two homes for the last year. His mom, Nancy, found him to be withdrawn, sullen and sad when Charley came to her home after being with his dad, Phil. Nancy and Phil believed in the Kids First philosophy of co-parenting and so they discussed this behavior. They agreed Phil would schedule a really fun trip the next time Charley was with him.

Charley was a big Red Sox fan so Phil got some tickets to the next game. Father and son had a great time at the baseball game. They ate hot dogs, sat behind the players' dugout and cheered to a Red Sox victory at the end.

When Charley returned to Nancy, he arrived in the same sad mood. Nancy asked, "Didn't you do lots of cool things when you were with Dad? Charley answered, "Yes, is that all right?" Nancy put her arms around Charley and told him, "It's OK with me that you love Dad. I want you to have a good time with him. It is not that I won't miss you, but I know it is important for you to have a good relationship with him." Until that event, Nancy never realized how important it was to support Phil in order to provide support to Charley.

Parents who support their kids' transitions:

- Do not use that transition to ask probing questions about the personal life of the other parent.

- Are positive and listen well to whatever information the child may want to share.

- Say 'hello' to the other parent and whomever he/she is with.

- Are on time.

Kids Say: Don't fight over us like objects. Treat us like persons.

Practical transition ideas

- Adopt a business-like approach. Greet the other parent as one would greet a colleague.

- Have at least one co-parenting conversation per week to inform the other parent of events/issues/schedules in preparation for the transition.

- Develop some rules for transitions to make them as stress-free as possible, such as the receiving parent always picks up the child.

- Establish a plan for the initial re-entry to each home. For example: a few minutes to decompress in the child's room, some time spent playing alone or whatever helps the child re-connect with the space and atmosphere of the environment.

- Do not talk about legal proceedings or financial matters in front of the kids.

- Cut some slack for the other parent. Everyone is feeling stress, and it mostly affects the kids.

- Practice some starter words to make it easier to greet the other parent in a reasonable way.

    o (On the phone) "Is this a good time to talk?

    o (In person) "Bobby got an A on his last math test." Or, some other positive remark about the child.

Understanding a reluctant traveler

When a child does not want to go to the other parent, a helpful parent acknowledges the child's sad feelings, but is firm and positive about the importance of the child's relationship with the other parent. Kids may fuss about many different transitions in their lives, such as going to school or to the dentist.

It is not unusual for kids to complain to <u>both</u> parents about not wanting to go to the <u>other</u> parent's home in order to show their loyalty to the parent they are leaving. Caring parents present clear and loving direction in spite of their children's reluctance.

A comforting transition ritual

Donald was a family therapist who counseled many separating parents over the years. He frequently told them about the method he used to help his kids transition back to his home after he was separated from their mom.

"The transition usually occurred in the late afternoon. Their mom and I agreed that the parent who last had residence with the kids would be the parent to deliver them for the transition. When the kids arrived, I greeted them and welcomed them to join me in the kitchen when they felt settled in. Transition day was always pizza day. I had balls of dough prepared along with favorite sauces and toppings.

"Whenever the kids felt ready to join me, each would venture into the kitchen where we would knead the fresh dough balls. The kitchen counter was long so we didn't actually face each other, but we worked side by

side, *pounding away at the dough, sometimes more vigorously than others!*

"By the time we were ready to roll out the dough and apply the sauces, all four of us would be in the kitchen, comparing notes about who could best toss the pizza crust and who wanted which toppings. There were usually plenty of laughs, but sometimes it was just peaceful. Kids were free to talk about their time away from me, or they could just talk about the pizza.

"On most occasions, the kids would gradually open up with stories about what happened while they were away from me. I'd listen mostly and ask few questions, except in response to their stories. By the time we were all sitting down to pizza, we were feeling pretty comfortable with each other. It was always the same routine and it turned into a beloved, family ritual.

"The kids are all grown now, but when they come to visit me with their own kids, they always want to begin by making pizza."

Chapter Seven

Holidays and Celebrations
(*Feasts or Fights?*)

Plan, plan, plan

Family celebrations and holiday events are ripe with emotions and expectations, running the gamut from eager anticipation to dread. In addition, separated families need to deal with endless logistical and personal complications. There is no easy way out, and there is no right answer, but planning and predictability will help kids cope.

- **Begin early**

Kids love holidays. Families generally are sentimentally attached to their holiday traditions. Since some part of these family holiday rituals will be lost upon the parents' separation, parents should take holiday planning seriously. Separating parents take a positive step toward re-stabilizing family rituals by planning for them up front, when they begin writing out their separation plans. Successful holiday schedules cannot be left until the holiday is close at hand.

- **Be specific**

Kids want to know what to expect year after year at holiday time. They are comforted to repeat a pattern. New rituals replace old ones, but a ritual never develops if it needs to be renegotiated every year. Specific and detailed holiday plans will provide kids with the security of knowing they have a plan they can count on. Even the most amicable separation is benefited by a written document containing specific holiday details, confirmed and finalized by the parents. Future events can never be foreseen entirely.

• Include the kids

Despite occasional complaints to the contrary, kids want their parents to be in charge of major decisions. However, they also want to have a voice in decisions that concern their happiness, and they want that voice to be heard. Based upon the ages of the kids, parents are wise to include kids in discussions of new holiday traditions, while making it clear that the final decision will be up to the parents.

Kids Say: Check with the kids before making decisions about them.

• Be open and flexible

Though parents are urged to specify a very detailed schedule for holiday events, it is also unrealistic to block out the possibility of changes. A schedule for a 2 year old is likely to be inappropriate for a 13 year old. Step-families and new partners may be part of future holidays and adjustments will be required. However, the same rules of planning, specificity, predictability and inclusion of kids apply.

Managing the emotions of holidays

• Create new traditions

It is OK, even important, to acknowledge that "something has changed this year" as families go through the first holidays following separations. Each parent can play a role to help create a new, personalized tradition that honors the old traditions.

• Parents' reflections

It is healthy for parents to spend some time sorting out their own expectation, hopes and fears for the holidays. Parents are likely to have strong feelings about the other parent. The first year is tough. This is a time for parents to have low expectations while maintaining a "let's make the best of it" attitude.

• Experiences at the other home

Parents respect their kids' need for privacy by not asking probing questions about the other parent's home. However, kids may want to discuss their holiday experiences and they will feel comfortable if they are free to do so. The kids' holiday experience is an amalgam of all the events. When kids feel free to discuss their experiences at the other home, it helps them integrate their own personal holiday memories.

Holiday don'ts

• No surprises

Introduction of surprises or emotionally charged information is best delayed until a quieter time. For example, introducing new friends or partners to the kids at holiday times borders on overload and threatens the stability of the holiday celebration. Sharing of important news, such as moving, should occur as much as possible prior to the holidays or may need to wait until after. When parents keep in mind the child's point of view during holidays, they can avoid bad perceptions of otherwise good news.

- ### No issues

Refrain from the temptation to use holiday drop-off and pick-up times to review past problems and areas of tension. Parents can easily project their own feelings onto their child.

Kids Say: Don't tell your kids that you are separating near a major holiday because that creates associations that will last a long time.

Special events and anniversaries

Periodic recurrences of feelings of pain and loss happen even after parents and kids seem to have resolved many sad feelings. These recurrences frequently happen at sensitive times of special events and anniversaries. Parents are wise to prepare themselves by being alert to their own feelings and keeping in mind the effects on the kids at the following times:

- Parents' wedding anniversary or other memorable family occasions

- Religious ceremonies
  (Bar Mitzvah, First Communion, etc.)

- Remarriage of one of the co-parents
- Birth of a child to a co-parent
- Graduations
- Marriages of children
- Births of grandchildren

No right answer

It should be expected that difficult feelings and behaviors will arise around holidays and special events. Unfortunately, parents do not have a guidebook that tells them what to do for every such event. There is only a right solution for a specific family and specific kids. Informed, caring parents work together to figure out what works to put kids first.

Chapter Eight

Parental Anger
(The Fight the Kids Don't Want to See)

Conflict between two parents can have an irreparable impact on their children. Anger is the heart and soul of most problems during and after separation and divorce. Yet anger is a normal response to change, loss and grief. When a parent understands his or her own anger and its source, kids are less likely to suffer.

Sources of parents' anger

Separation is frequently accompanied by fear and anger. Parents do not have to look far for opportunities to be angry during this sensitive time. Meanwhile, kids need their parents to work in harmony. Understanding adult anger during separation may help to put kids first.

- **Pain**

Anger is a common way to deal with powerful feelings like sadness, hurt, loss, loneliness and guilt. For many, it is easier to feel angry than to cry and feel very sad.

- **Power**

Anger is a way to feel powerful and in control instead of feeling powerless and out of control.

- **Avoidance**

    Anger is a way to avoid looking at one's own problems in the relationship. It is much easier to blame the other parent and focus on his or her shortcomings rather than looking at oneself.

- **Exit strategy**

    Anger is a way to leave. It is easier to let go of a person you hate than one you still have good feelings about. One parent may make the other into a bad villain, reshaping memories into dark, negative images. Altered, bad images are devastating for children who want to admire and respect both parents.

- **Connection**

    Anger is a way to stay connected to the other parent. As long as strong feelings of anger still preoccupy one's thoughts, then that parent has not yet let go of the attachment to the other.

    Anger is a way to connect to other people. Friends and relatives may be more than ready to side with one parent against the other. Having a common enemy can create friends and reduce the sense of isolation.

- **Adversarial Process**

    The legal system is based on an adversarial model. It may feed anger by focusing on good vs. bad or right vs. wrong. More often than not there are only shades of gray. Even well-intentioned family therapists may ally against the other parent when they hear only one parent's side of the story.

Kids Say: No yelling, insults or swearing in front of the kids. Yell outside if you have to!

How parents' anger affects kids

Lindsay was ten years old when she started alternating weeks between her mom and dad's homes ever since they divorced five years ago. Mom and Dad agreed on little; they seldom communicated; and they each boasted about different values.

Lindsay's mom thought girls should participate in sports to develop physical capabilities and learn how to work together as a team. She disapproved of the musical career chosen by Lindsay's dad because he never earned enough money.

Lindsay's dad is an accomplished musician who was delighted that his daughter had musical talent. He thought sports was a waste of time and led to injuries and hyper-competition.

When Lindsay was staying at her mom's house, she played the role of athlete. She attended soccer practice in the fall and lacrosse in the spring. When Lindsay stayed with her dad, she was a fledgling saxophone player. He accompanied her on piano and took her to regular music lessons.

Lindsay managed to hide her other extracurricular activities from the disapproving parent for almost two years. Though she is a talented music student and a competent athlete, at age 14 she now suffers from depression and eating disorders.

Kids Say: Don't put us in the middle!

- **Divided loyalty**

  Kids whose parents have significant unresolved conflicts feel caught in the middle between parents. This divided loyalty may result in a child's rejecting one parent in order to stay loyal to the other (and there is no way to predict which one will be rejected).

- **Kids as therapists**

  Kids need to be kids; and, parents can promote that by avoiding the temptation to use their children as close confidantes. Kids can feel great pressure to resolve their parents' conflict, denying their own feelings, thoughts and needs. Conflict is for adults to manage, not kids.

- **Taking sides**

  When kids hear one parent blaming or being negative about the other, they feel forced to take sides. Children identify with both parents, so asking them to choose one over the other causes extreme anxiety. They feel pulled in two directions at once. Their relationship with both parents is negatively affected.

Kids Say: Sometimes we feel crazy, but we hide it.

- **Self-worth**

    Conflict between parents may reduce a child's own sense of worth. Kids identify with their parents. When one parent expresses negative feelings and anger towards the other, the child takes it personally. This may translate into fears of losing a parent's love if they look like, act like, or have characteristics of that other parent.

- **Role models**

    Parents in unresolved conflict fail to teach children appropriate tools for dealing with anger. Kids may be overly aggressive or overly compliant to avoid having any conflict take place. They fail to develop conflict resolution skills.

Kids Say: Don't let your anger show in front of the kids.

Anger's long-term effects

- ### Conflict lasts through the generations

A family therapist recounts how his parents' divorce and separation continues to haunt his children:

> *"My kids just went to their cousin's graduation where their grandparents would be, that is their grandmother, their grandfather and his second wife of 25 years. The two women can not—will not—associate with one another. They could barely be at my wedding together and here they were at this granddaughter's graduation from college and they still would not associate.*

> *"They would not sit together to do the right thing for this young woman who was graduating. So, my kids come home with stories about how they spent this time with this one and this time with that one. And, oh, it got a little dicey at this point because 'we thought we had time alone with this one, but then the other one showed up early and she wasn't supposed to.' This is blossoming out into the whole world with grandparents, relatives, friends that all have opinions. My kids see that. They deal with it. They have to live with it. That becomes their life."*

When parents hold on to anger and engage in conflict, they risk establishing a pattern which will affect generations to come with unhappiness and discomfort. Kids do not want this to be the legacy from their parents or their grandparents.

- ### Anger affects memories

Ed told a high school graduation story about his daughter, Charlene. Charlene's mom called him shortly before the graduation and told him it was <u>her</u> day with Charlene and he'd better not show up. "If you come, I will call my attorney," was her final threat.

Ed did not go to the graduation. When Charlene asked how come he wasn't there, he just said, "I'm really sorry that I couldn't be there, but Mom and I talked about it. It was her day and we just didn't want any conflict there for you, but I am so proud of you."

Ed broke the conflict. Ed waived the opportunity to tell his daughter how unfair her mother was. If Ed had given into the temptation of full disclosure, he would only have created an angry scene negatively impacting the graduation.

Charlene was fortunate to have a dad courageous enough to disengage from conflict. On the other hand, Charlene did not have her dad at her graduation.

Kids want courageous parents who will:

- Disengage from anger.
- Avoid making new friends who fuel the conflict.
- Avoid therapists who support anger against the other parent.
- Avoid attorneys who encourage litigation to punish the other parent.

Chapter Nine

New Relationships, New Families
(*More Characters—More Complexity*)

Despite what some adults believe, children usually do not feel relief from divorce (although in some cases, children say they are relieved to be out of the fray and away from on-going conflict). Children often have a strong desire for their parents to get back together. In addition, adjustments to new adult partners or their children are just more obstacles for children to overcome. Thus, kids need more time than a parent might suspect to adjust to household changes caused by the separation. Parents are generally ahead of their children in all stages of the separation and divorce process.

> *When Caleb's parents told him they were getting a divorce because they just couldn't live together any-more, he was angry. "Whenever I fight with my sister they tell me I have to work it out. How come they don't have to work it out? It's not fair!" (Caleb, 13)*

Looking back to move forward

Before addressing a new relationship, it is important for a parent to look back and assess how far they have come emotionally and physically. Has the parent processed their emotions surrounding separation and loss? Has the parent adequately guided the children through their grief and subsequent life changes? Has the family unit settled into a fairly permanent home? Has the parent found financial stability and independence? Answers to questions like these help parents determine readiness for a new relationship.

Go slowly

The first year after the parents' separation is the most sensitive time. Kids need a great deal of their parents' attention. The absence of one parent in the kids' daily lives may cause kids to fear about their day-to-day needs being met. Kids may become afraid of being abandoned.

Therefore, dating or introducing a new partner is best delayed until the kids' lives have achieved a comfortable level of stability. Parents who are excited by the prospect of a new romance are frequently unable to be objective judges of their child's readiness for the new relationship. Parents may lose their perspective and try to make the transition too quickly. When a parent focuses on a new love or a busy dating schedule, the kids may fear for their own place in the parent's affection.

Kids Say: Don't ignore the kids just because you have a new friend.

Dating

Parents' discussions with their children about dating will depend upon the ages and circumstances of the kids. Good judgment is required to introduce the concept of a parent's dating and the fact that the date may develop into a new relationship. Too often, anxious parents are looking for opportunities to validate their dating activities, rather than considering how hard this step is for their kids.

Kids want to know it is safe for them to discuss their feelings about their parents' dating. They want reassurance that the parent will not desert them for another relationship. Some kids may be upset because they harbor a fantasy that their parents will get back together. Additionally, introduction of a new significant adult creates a loyalty bind for children between the new adult and the left behind parent.

When it is time to integrate a new partner into family activities, the introduction should be gradual and kids' reactions should be closely monitored. Child-centered activities, like a picnic or amusements, make the introduction easier. If kids react negatively, parents should consider waiting longer rather than forcing the integration. This is an important time for parents to spend one-on-one time with each of their kids.

It is best to delay having a new partner sleep over until approximately one year after separation or until the divorce is final, and limit overnights to times when the children are not in the home. However, if a new partner does spend the night, a parent needs to plan carefully beforehand. Ideally, the other parent is consulted and considered. Next, the kids are notified and their responses need to be respected, including delaying the event until kids feel more comfortable. Then, moving slowly, the parent observes kids' reactions and adjusts behavior if appropriate. Adolescents may be particularly resistant to a new adult in their home.

Co-habitation and/or remarriage

Subsequent families are structurally and emotionally different from first families. Children and adults often experience upset and sadness as they react to the loss of their old, familiar ways. Caring relationships usually take a long time to evolve.

High expectations of instant love between a new partner or a step-parent and future stepchildren can lead to many disappointments. If the step-family relationships are allowed to develop at a pace that is comfortable for all those involved, then caring between step-relatives has a greater opportunity to develop.

A Word about Discipline

Children do not usually accept discipline from a stepparent until a significant amount of positive relationship building has occurred. This can be from 18 months to 2 years depending on the family. The best advice is for the primary parents to maintain the disciplinarian role as the new stepfamily develops. However, if the stepparent is temporarily left in charge, the biological parent should clarify that the stepparent may enforce the house rules.

New siblings

If a new partner comes to the relationship with children, extra caution is required. Relationships between step-siblings vary tremendously due to ages, personalities and gender. Some children become extremely close and supportive over time; some stay highly competitive; some ignore each other.

Changes in birth order of the step-siblings may have a particularly disruptive effect on kids. For example, the oldest child may no longer be the oldest in a blended family. Old patterns and ways of perceiving oneself may undergo adjustment, sometimes painfully.

A new baby in the family may be a joyful event, but also adds a layer of complexity. Kids' feelings of displacement should be considered. Step-families are frequently more successful when they try to work out and develop new family patterns, while preserving some old customs. However, all family members need to be reminded that new patterns take time, patience and ingenuity to develop successfully.

Integrating a step-family with teenagers can be particularly difficult. Adolescents are gradually moving away from their families as part of normal development, while needing a secure base to return to. They also have a longer previous family history. Teens want to feel they have a strong voice in step-family negotiations. Sometimes that voice is used to let parents know the teens are going to withdraw from many of the family activities.

Kids Say: We were shoved into this new household; we were the outsiders.

"My mom and step-dad thought we were going to be the Brady Bunch when they first got married. It made us all want to run and hide. Once they stopped trying to

force us together, we actually got to know each other better." (Stacey, 15)

• The occasional kids

When kids' residential schedules provide that they spend only brief periods in the non-residential parent's household, they frequently feel uncomfortable, like outsiders. They experience vastly different adjustments than the kids who live there all the time. Some ideas to make them feel more connected include:

- Engaging in whole-family fun activities,
- Assigning simple chores,
- Requesting participation in a family project,
- Allowing the child's friends to visit at the same time, and
- Informing kids in advance about planned activities.

The left-behind parent

When one parent has a new partner and the other parent is alone, divided loyalties often present difficulties for kids. They may resist relating to another parental figure in their lives. Both parents can help a child deal with his or her loyalty bind with the other parent in a variety of ways:

- Giving the child permission to love all of the adults in their life.
- Recognizing and acknowledging the child's feelings.
- Acknowledging the loyalty bind the child is feeling.

- Complimenting the other parent minimizes the child's need to be overly protective; criticizing the left-behind parent fully fuels the loyalty conflict the child experiences.

Rejection of a step-parent may have nothing to do with the personal characteristics of the step-parent. Warm and loving step-parents may actually exacerbate the loyalty conflict felt by children. Over time, it becomes easier for children and patient parents to understand there can never be too much love. Fondness for a step-parent does not need to diminish love for a parent.

Kids Say: I felt guilty not being with my mother, who was alone.

Talking with kids about co-habitation or remarriage

- **How to engage the conversation**

    - The first time, tell all the kids at the same time.

    - Tell the other biological parent either just before or just after you tell the kids. Do not make the child the messenger.

    - Tell the kids that the other biological parent knows (or will soon know).

    - Expect that each child will have different questions, feelings and reactions. Respond to each individually.

- Be candid. If you do not have an answer, say so.

- **The Most Important Messages to Convey to Kids**

  - Both parents will continue to love you, just the same as before.

  - Both parents will still spend quality time with you just as before. (If this is not true, explain the reason and provide lots of reassurance.)

  - This may feel exciting sometimes and hard at other times. This is normal. It probably will help if you tell adults how you are feeling about the changes.

  - Parents always want to hear what you think about these changes and how they are affecting you, even if you think they will not like what you have to say.

  - In the end, you will have more people who care about you than you did before.

- **Practical steps toward new family adjustment**

  - Move one step at a time to make changes, and don't force it.

  - Empathize. Creating a stepfamily is difficult for every person, no matter their age.

  - Be respectful whenever dealing with the other biological parent, and convey assurance that a new relationship will not interfere with their co-parenting partner's continuing role.

  - Sometimes smaller is better. One-on-one time helps to maintain existing relationships and deepen new ones. This includes parent and child, step-parent and step-child, biological parent and child, and biological parent and step-parent.

- Be aware that inappropriate sexual behavior occurs at a higher rate in step-families. Biologic incest taboos are reduced between the step-siblings and also step-parent and step-child. It may be best to keep overt displays of affection between the adults to a minimum, at first. Protect family members' right to privacy.

- Create new rules and new rituals for the new family, while maintaining elements from each of the prior families.

- Find family activities in which everyone is at ease whenever possible.

- Step-parents often need to function as an adult friend rather than a new parent, especially with older children.

- A step-parent may be the adult in charge and may enforce the rules of the house, but that person is still not the parent.

- Step-parents are usually more successful carving out roles for themselves that are different from, and do not compete with, the biological parents.

- The new couple needs time for themselves to create a foundation for the new family unit.

- The new couple presents a unified front. It is never a good idea for kids to know they can divide and conquer.

- All of the steps required for effective co-parenting (as set forth in Chapter 3) are even more important for effective step-parenting.

- Attend a step-family educational program like the Kids First Program or similar program for step-parents.

"For Dennis and me, bedtime was the most difficult time of the day. My girls always treasured bedtime stories with me on my bed and didn't want to share this ritual. With a little creativity and a lot of support from Dennis, we found something that works. Now Dennis and I alternate nighttime stories on the 'big bed' with our own kids. We found a way to keep my family ritual without diminishing our step-family as a whole. And now Dennis' kids have new special time with their dad."

New Opportunities for Growth and Love

When a parent commits to a new relationship, he or she is also making a choice for their children and for the other co-parent. Since most co-parents are connected through their children for a lifetime, it serves everyone if the parents communicate and cooperate for the benefit of their children. Despite the challenges of a new relationship, there will be a deep sense of satisfaction as the family starts to work together. Kids get a unique perspective on life; learning that individuals with different backgrounds can live together in peace; observing more adult role models; having opportunities from new sibling interactions; and more birthday presents! Creating a stepfamily where the members truly appreciate each other is not easy, but the rewards are well worth the effort.

Chapter Ten

The Legal System
(Courts, Lawyers and Kids)

The power and authority of the court

• State laws govern

Laws regarding parental rights and responsibilities vary from state to state. Individual state laws address child support obligations and provide guidelines for what is in the best interest of children. Parents who have been married can file for a divorce decree which will order property interests and spousal support (if any) as well child-related issues. If parents are unmarried, either parent may file a motion to determine parental rights and responsibilities. The rights of same sex parents are not so clearly defined at this time.

• The good

Courts appreciate and support parents who agree on how to structure a healthy post-separation life for their children. Courts frequently provide parents with guidelines and resources for working together to reach agreement.

A court order helps to provide stability and predictability for all family members. Child support is established according to state guidelines and both parents must strictly abide by the terms. Issues of residence, schedule and holidays are stated in varying degrees of specificity, depending on factors such as the parents' desires, the attorneys involved or the judge approving the order.

A court order which addresses all foreseeable circumstances can be an extraordinarily useful tool for the kids' benefit. If parents agree to be flexible, they are free to make schedule changes accordingly. However, if a dispute arises, a court order with specific provisions can resolve the argument. Any deviation from the order can take place only if both parents agree.

• The bad

Courts operate as an adversarial system. When two litigants in a car crash argue that it was the other person's fault, they each focus on all the ways they were right and the other person was wrong. On leaving the courtroom, they can scowl at each other and go their separate ways.

When courts need to resolve issues for parents, the resulting adversarial process encourages parents to embellish their own "wisdom and goodness" and to exaggerate the "ignorance and incapacity" of the other parent. But when parents leave the courtroom, they still have to figure out who is going to pick up the kids from the sitter.

• The ugly

Protracted court involvement for making decisions about kids is very damaging to kids and their parents. When the adversarial system kicks in fully, everyone gets bruised and resentful.

How Kids Are Affected by Legal Battles

- Kids are exposed to raw hostility between the two people they love and need most.

- Kids are uncertain, fearful about "what will happen to me" in the future.

- Kids do not want to go to court; they worry that what they say will hurt one of their parents.

- Kids lose the benefit of two parents who can honestly communicate to each other; weakness or problems may be used as ammunition in court.

- The cost of extensive litigation is colossal and puts a huge financial strain on parents and kids.

- Kids lose their parents' focus when parents must direct their attention toward their position in the litigation.

Paul was angry and going through a high-conflict divorce. He and Denise had spent three long sessions trying to negotiate all of their divorce issues. He felt Denise just wouldn't agree to anything he wanted.

Paul ranted to his co-worker one day, "I'm going to get half."

"Half of what?"

Paul went on a tirade, "Half of everything—half of the money, half of the property, half of the time."

Paul had ceased concentrating on his kids' well-being. He was in the legal system and he was going to use it to get "his half" of the kids, regardless of what that meant for them. It would take the Wisdom of Solomon to know how to deliver half a kid!

The role of the lawyers

- **On the plus side**

    Lawyers can play a constructive role for separating parents, including:

    - Advising parents of their rights and responsibilities
    - Explaining how the law affects their options
    - Providing useful information about successful parenting plans that other parents have implemented
    - Assisting with negotiations
    - Drafting a well thought-out settlement agreement
    - Preparing all legal documents for a smooth journey through the court system
    - Foreseeing long term implications of the plans

    In some circumstances, one of the most helpful roles of an attorney is telling the attorney's own client when he or she is off base. Clients feel comfortable having someone they can trust to look out for their interests. However, sometimes the biggest favor a lawyer can do is to take the client out of the comfort zone by pointing out an unreasonable or unrealistic position which is not in the interest of the kids.

As an example, Jane Doe may go to her attorney saying that she needs to have full-time residence with her kids. She knows their needs best because she has always tended to them. Their father, John, is wrapped up in his work and his new girl friend. He does not have a good home for them and is not a good influence on the kids. So, Jane wants her attorney to argue that the kids can be with their dad every other Sunday afternoon. Phone calls can take place to him weekly.

If Jane Doe's attorney had attended the Kids First Family Law Seminar, the advice of a local district court judge would provide guidance in a case like Jane's. Judge Smith explained how he applies the state statute requiring judges to make decisions about children according to "Best Interest of the Child" factors. The judge stated:

"When two capable parents present a question of where a child should live, I think the most important factor of analysis is how each of the parents facilitates the relationship between the other parent and the child. For me that is #1. Whichever parent is not doing that is the parent I really scrutinize.

"I sometimes say to parents that having primary residence means having the child most of the time, which really is an issue of trust. The court is trusting

you and expects that you will encourage your child's relationship with the other parent."

Jane Doe's attorney would make some investigation into his client's claims to see if John Doe was as bad an influence as his client states. If John is a reasonably capable, loving parent who is interested in establishing a close, post-separation relationship with his children, Jane's attorney may have to educate her about the legal risk inherent in her position. If she is lucky, Jane would also receive some education from her lawyer about why it is important for kids to spend meaningful time with both parents.

Kids Say: Kids should be able to call and write the parent they are not living with.

• Throwing fuel on the fire

Unfortunately for the kids, some parents look for attorneys who will fight for their clients' positions, regardless of the reasonableness of that position and regardless of the potential harm to the kids. Some parents think having a bully for an attorney will help them scare off the other parent or score a win in court. Well-intentioned attorneys may not mean to cause harm to children, but unless they grasp the concepts underlying the psychological and emotional well-being of kids, they may handle parental rights litigation the same way as car accident litigation.

All attorneys have an obligation to zealously advocate for their clients. They must go through various stages of discovery, which may include intrusive interrogatories, investigations or depositions. One parent described it as a system "based on suspicion and distrust." Actually, the discovery process is the attorney's way of making sure his/her client is making decisions based on substantiated, factual information.

However, the role of attorneys in parental rights cases can be abused. If a parent is hell-bent on winning at any price, that parent will be able to find an attorney who will fight with aggressiveness and rancor for just about anything that parent wants, regardless of its benefit for kids.

• Remaining in charge

Parents who want to put kids first following a separation will look for an attorney who respects their interest in making the well being of their children the first priority.

Once the parent identifies and hires an attorney who shares this priority, the parent can still monitor the attorney's actions. If negotiations are heating up and causing strife between the parents, a client is free to instruct the attorney to try to cool things off. After all, at the end of a nasty day of negotiations, the attorney goes home to his/her own family while the client has to continue dealing with the other parent.

Kids Say: Don't tell me everything about the divorce negotiations. Only tell me things about how I relate to each parent.

- **Finding an attorney**

Kids do not want to know about their parents' attorneys. Kids just want their parents to be peaceful and supportive of their relationship with both parents. Whatever attorney helps with those goals is good for kids.

Parents who are separating put their kids first by considering the following when selecting a potential attorney to help them through the process:

- Be clear and direct about what style of approach is desired.

- State primary goals and those which are less important.

- Watch out for a lawyer who says, "I will get you exactly what you want."

- Beware of proposed tactics that create needless hostility.

- Look for assistance finding a fair solution for family harmony.

- **Questions for a prospective attorney who will put kids first.**

    - What percentage of your practice is family law?

    - What percentage of your cases involving child issues settle versus going to court?

    - When, if ever, do you think child issues should go to court?

    - How do you usually proceed if there are issues regarding children?

    - Do you encourage parents to talk to each other about child-related issues?

    - What professional organizations do you belong to?

    - Are you trained and/or experienced with mediation?

Most states have internet sites for information about divorce and separation.

> Judges Say: *Usually when I am forced to make a decision, everyone is unhappy.*

Approaches to try before going to court

- **Private agreement and negotiation**

    Some parents are able to talk between themselves, or with the help of a therapist, and reach agreement on all issues regarding their children. Their agreement can be written and presented to the court for approval. If possible, it is prudent for each party to consult with an attorney to review the written document to make sure the language of the agreement is legally valid and clear enough to properly implement the parental decisions made.

• Mediation

Most states require or recommend mediation if there is an issue in dispute regarding children. Even in the absence of a dispute, many parents find it helpful to discuss co-parenting with the assistance of a skilled mediator who is familiar with separation issues.

Family-focused mediators have many different backgrounds. With proper investigation, parents can select the right combination of temperament, attitude, cost, experience or specific skill set, such as a mediator with a legal or mental health background. The choice depends on the comfort and needs of the parents. Some mediators will also draft a settlement agreement, though most suggest the parties consult with their own individual attorneys before presenting it to the court.

• Custody evaluations (Guardians *ad litem)*

Depending on the state law, courts may appoint, or a parent may request the appointment of an experienced professional to make a recommendation to the court as to what is in the best interest of a child (frequently called custody evaluators or guardians *ad litem*, and referred to as "evaluators" in this section). Some courts provide evaluators for difficult cases; some evaluators work on a volunteer basis. Usually, parents pay the fees for hiring the evaluator that they agree upon or as ordered by the court.

Custody evaluators are obligated to follow the state laws to determine what is in the best interest of the child. They have varying powers for their investigation depending on the state. Frequently, they are authorized by the court to meet and interview: the children, the parents, teachers and other school personnel, daycare providers, physicians, relatives and other people with whom the children come into contact. After all investigations, the evaluator makes recommendations for the parents and the court as to what parental arrangement is in the best interest of the child. The court is not obligated to accept all aspects of the evaluator's report, but the evaluator is usually a persuasive voice since he or she is the most objective party focused on the best interest of the child.

Many custody evaluators work with parents to try to bring them to agreement on a parenting plan. Sometimes, parents will reach agreement, with or without the assistance of lawyers, based on the evaluator's report. Once parents see what is going to be recommended to the court, they have more incentive to reach agreement between themselves.

Custody evaluations are considered a good alternative to having children testify in court. Judges normally want to avoid the heartbreaking scenes of children dragged in to the court room to talk about their parents.

> **Kids Say:** When brought into judges' chambers during a custody dispute, most often kids say, 'Tell them [my parents] to stop fighting,' or, 'Tell them to stop criticizing the other in front of me.'

- **Arbitration**

Parents who are unable to agree on child issues, despite their efforts to mediate, may agree to be bound by the decision of a privately selected arbitrator. Arbitrators for child issues are usually family law attorneys who have experience with the court system and the laws of the state governing such matters. Parties contract for their arbitration hearing to be held on a specific date, with the arbitrator they select. Sometimes, the parties may elect to have a less formal arbitration without strict adherence to the rules of evidence used by the courts.

Contested court hearings

If all other efforts to resolve the parenting issues fail, then the parties with their attorneys go before a judge and present evidence favorable to their point of view.

The job of the other attorney at this point is to tear apart your ideas, and discredit you, so his or her client will win this court battle.

Contested hearings sometimes last for several days, and they always cost thousands of dollars. Everyone ends up feeling bruised and angry, and usually no one is happy with the result. After all, how can a judge, a stranger in a black robe, make a better decision about the kids' welfare than the kids' parents?

Parents who put their kids' needs first resolve the parenting issues of their case in a way other than a contested court hearing.

Kids Want:
- Whatever process helps parents concentrate their efforts on their children's adjustment, and;

- Whatever process results in a long-term healthy relationship with both parents!

Chapter Eleven

Schools Supporting the Co-Parenting Process
(Working With Children Undergoing Family Transition)

Schools have the monumental task of providing education for the youth of the community, as well as providing opportunities for positive socialization, physical health and good citizenship. Schools are mandated to achieve higher and higher levels of test-scores, while also helping children develop a multitude of other skills—from honesty and respect to conflict resolution and healthy choices. Some say the schools are being asked to take over more jobs that used to be the responsibility of the parents.

An additional layer of complexity arises when classrooms are populated with kids experiencing family transitions. Kids may have difficulty focusing on academics when parents are in conflict, residences are changing, and new family members are being added and subtracted at home.

Signs to look for in children whose families are experiencing transition

School personnel may observe the following signs and indications from children whose families are experiencing transition:

- Confusion about what day they are supposed to go to daycare or mom's or dad's house, which parent is picking them up, or what bus they are supposed to take home.

- Worry about their parents while they are at school.

- Worry about their parents arguing when they exchange the children.

- A decrease in grades.

- An increase in aggressive, rebellious, or acting out behavior.

- An increase in withdrawn or isolative behavior.

- More trips to the school nurse with complaints of bellyaches and headaches.

- More requests to leave the classroom to go to the bathroom, get a drink, etc.

- Daydreaming in class

- Irritability

- Difficulty getting along with peers

- Children not having what they need when they come to school, such as homework being left at the other parent's house

How teachers and schools can educate parents about school issues during family transitions

In order to help kids when such signs appear, schools need assistance from the parents. Parents may be embarrassed or reluctant to share family changes. However, a good parent handbook will inform parents that when family transitions occur, it is important that parents communicate with the school to help their children by doing the following:

- Inform school personnel when a family change is about to or has recently occurred.

- Consult with school personnel about signs that a child is having difficulty.

- Inform school personnel of parenting schedules and keep the school updated of any changes to this, especially when bus changes occur.

- Make sure that the child's emergency form lists all the adults who may be picking up the child.

- Inform school personnel when a new person/people move into the home or if the child moves into someone else's home. Step-family situations can be very difficult for kids.

- Make sure that children have all of their necessities at each home, i.e. toothbrush, toiletries, clothes, shoes, etc.

- Using a child's backpack as a delivery tool for notes or money between parents is frequently uncomfortable for children. Strongly consider using an alternate communication system.

What teachers and schools can do to better serve kids whose families are experiencing transition

• Create boundaries to protect kids

Schools can set clear boundaries for parents when they attempt to engage in conflict in front of their children at school. At parent conferences, school personnel can help children by encouraging co-parenting and not to allowing parents to denigrate each other. They can remain neutral in order to avoid being drawn into taking sides between parents. If there is conflict between the parents, school personnel can set up separate conferences for each parent.

Mr. Jones is a high school guidance counselor who frequently works with kids discussing their college plans. He recounted the story of a recently separated mom and dad who accompanied their daughter, Jill, to a meeting at his office to discuss finances and selections of colleges.

Dad sat almost outside the door while Mom and Jill were practically on top of each other at my desk. Mom proceeded to say that although Dad was "loaded," he refused to give any money and, therefore, Jill would not be able to go to a reputable college. Mom said she wanted to know the options. However, before I could finish my first sentence, Mom continued the attack and vicious slurs against Dad. He remained detached, saying just a few words here and there. I asked Jill what her plans were. She was dejected and it was clear that what she really wanted to say, but she could not say out loud, was that she just wanted to get away. Instead, Jill talked awkwardly and tried not take sides.

Jill was a junior when the meeting took place. I said the most important thing for Jill was to finish school and focus on her academics. I told the parents that the financial conversation needed to take place between the two of them first and that it was detrimental to their daughter to be involved; their stress was reducing her chances of success. Jill looked visibly relieved. Mom tried to continue, but I said my services could not be utilized under these conditions and I politely brought the meeting to a close.

I think schools can help to protect kids from this sort of behavior. Kids are mortified when their parents do this. Often, school personnel feel browbeaten into accepting this kind of stuff and all too many parents are allowed to act out their dramas inappropriately. In Jill's senior year, I went through the college process with her and it was smooth and uneventful.

• Help kids whose families are experiencing transition

- School can be a respite for kids. Let the child know that you are there for them to talk to if they need to. You can also leave "the door" open by making general statements to the whole class that you are available to them if they need to talk.

- Create a space for kids to leave their overnight bags, sports equipment, etc. when they need to bring these things to school. Carrying these things from class to class can be very embarrassing for kids.

- Be sensitive at holiday and vacation times. These family events are frequently fraught with difficulty, especially for kids whose families are recently separated.

- Set up a mentoring program at your school whereby kids can obtain a list of potential adults or peers who are available to listen and lend support.

- Let the child know that the school social worker or guidance counselor can also be a support to them.

- Start family change/divorce groups at your school.

- Talk to parents about what resources are available to them and their children (such as Kids First or similar programs, etc.).

• Maintain communications and be respectful of confidentiality issues

- Make sure you are only speaking about a child to those people who are on the child's emergency phone list. Confidentiality issues tend to be very sensitive with families experiencing family transition.

- Arrange to have important documents and school information sent to separated or divorced parents at the two different addresses.

• Provide a list of books and other community resources for successful co-parenting during separation and divorce.

Chapter Twelve

One Child's Perspective
(Olivia's Story)

[This story was written by a young girl in Maine named Olivia when she was only 8 years old. She worked with a counselor to help her get through some of the most difficult parts of her parents' divorce, and one of the things that helped her the most was writing down her thoughts along the way. Four years later, Olivia has adjusted very well to the changes that divorce brought to her family and hopes that you can benefit from hearing her story.]

Life Changes!
By Olivia

Hello. My name is Olivia. I am 8 years old and I live in Maine. I am in the 3rd grade. My parents were separated from each other when I was 6 years old. This caused a lot of changes in my life that I had to get used to. Right now I live with my Mother but I see my Dad all the time too.

I decided to write this book for a few reasons. First, I wanted to help other kids deal with changes in their lives by sharing some of my ideas about the experiences in my life. Second, by writing this book, I can understand my own life changes a little better. Third, I would like to help other kids learn that there are ways to deal with changes that could happen in their lives, too.

1.   Separation and Divorce

Before my Mom and Dad got separated, I didn't know they were even talking about it. I was surprised when they told me. I thought when they were talking with each other, and they looked real serious, they were talking about normal stuff. When I found out about the separation, they told me together. I'm glad they did it that way.

On my Dad's last day at home, which I'll never forget, I felt very, very, very sad. I remember everything about it. My Dad felt sad too. He had to move to a different town and live with my Nana. After one year, he moved closer to me and now lives in an apartment in the next town from me. The ride to his house is only about 10 minutes away from where I live with my Mom.

After they were separated for a while and lived apart, they decided to officially get divorced. That means that they went to court and a judge signed a paper. This was a big Life Change!

2.   Giving Things Up

After my Mom and Dad got separated, my Mom and I moved into a new house where we couldn't have a dog unless we owned the house. We rented our new home so we had to find a new place for our dog. Her name is Chloe. I felt upset, sad and sort of mad that Chloe couldn't live with us anymore. She now lives in a different town in a house with our friends and their children. We still get to visit Chloe once in awhile (she officially still belongs to us), so that makes it easier. I didn't want to give my dog away but we couldn't live in our new place if we didn't. I miss her but I'm getting used to it now, and I found out that I can be okay without Chloe. Sometimes you have to give something up when Life Changes!

3. Some Things Change, Some Things Don't

After my Mom and Dad got separated and divorced, my Dad moved, my Mom and I moved, we gave up our dog, and I missed my Dad. These are all things that changed in my life. But there were lots of things that did not change. My Dad is still my Dad. My Mom is still my Mom. My Nana is still my Nana. My Gram is still my Gram. I still get to go to my same school. (Sometimes other kids have to move to a new town and start at a different school.) Even though I live in a new neighborhood, I still have the same friends at my school. I still do things with my Mom and with my Dad. But now sometimes we have to do them separately. Something that my parents have done to help me is that they have really had to keep talking to each other and have tried to get along. Sometimes not everything in Life Changes!

4. Taking Care of Myself

When Changes happened in my family, it took awhile to get used to them. It was hard at first to understand what was going on and what would happen next. For example, sometimes I missed my Dad a lot after he moved and I felt lonely without him. Things just weren't the same after he left. It took awhile to get used to this change. I began to be more afraid of things, like the dark, and sleeping on my own, and I wondered if I would be able to keep seeing my Dad. Talking with other people to understand what was happening was helpful. People that I talked with included my Social

Worker, and my parents. Some other people who are there for me if I need them are my grandmother, my grandfather, aunt, or my step-grandfather. It's important to talk about things that we are afraid of or confused about because we need to get answers and help. Questions are okay. Don't feel shy or worried about asking questions and trying to find answers.

I learned that it is important to take care of yourself when your parents get divorced, and I learned that they have to take care of themselves. Kids can't take care of their parents; they can only take care of themselves. Parents have to make their own decisions about separation and divorce; it's not up to the kids. Parents get divorced because of their own reasons, not because of their kids. Parents keep growing up too. Sometimes we get afraid of things in our lives when it feels different in our family, and it's important to talk to other people when Life Changes!

5. New Relationships

After a divorce, your parents may go on dates with a person that they have met somewhere. Sometimes parents will develop new relationships with new people, and you may be able to bond with that person too.

You may feel worried and confused about who will take care of you and what is going on. You may be angry at your parent because you may not know how to share your parent since it has been just you and your Mom or you and your Dad with undivided attention for each other. Or you may feel happy just to see your parent happy. You could feel all kinds of these feelings. But that is normal too, just remember Life Changes.

6. Three Years Later

As you all know, my name is Olivia, but I am now 9 and I will turn 10 in November. I am in third grade and I still go to the same school. I am still living with my parents divorced. Three years later I am used to it. I see my Dad almost every day. I now know how to deal with my feelings and I feel comfortable sharing them with others. Soon you will feel that too.

My Mom just went to Virginia on a business trip for four days. I am staying with my Dad and tonight, May 1st, I'm going to the airport with my aunt to pick up Mom. I can't wait.

My parents worked out a way to make sure I get equal attention from them both and that I would always be with an adult that could take care of me the way they do.

Sometimes parents with children get divorced, but they can work together to make sure you are well-taken care of.

A Note to Parents

Dear Parents,

As you can see, I worked through my parent's divorce because it was amicable. The most important thing they did to help me was they kept up their talking and their friendship. I still get the same attention that I got when my Mom and Dad were married.

I really had to get used to this change, in some ways it took apart my life. In three years I was able to sew my life back together. This is how your child can feel too if you as parents keep talking to each other and to your kids. Make sure that your children know why you got divorced, because they may think it's their fault like I did.

Sincerely,

Olivia

Appendix A

Effects of Divorce by Age

[Extracted from the first edition of the *Parent Handbook for Kids First: Parenting through Divorce* (Kids First Center, Inc., 1998)]

Please note: All children are individuals. This chart is not meant to imply that all children will behave or feel the same. Many children do, however, respond in ways similar to those described below.

FEELINGS/REACTIONS TO DIVORCE	WHAT TO DO
INFANTS – Birth to 1 year Infants may become either fussy or somewhat unresponsive. They may be harder to calm. They respond quickly to distress or depression in their parents. Disruption of sleeping/eating patterns is not uncommon.	If possible, infants need frequent contact with both parents. This allows them to maintain their attachment to both parents. They need relaxed time, where the parent is paying full attention. Ritual games (such as Peek-a-Boo) are a good way of doing this.

TODDLERS – 1 year to 30 months	Consider leaving something important to you with your toddler when you must leave them. Encourage them to do things for themselves, but if they need nurturing, give it freely. Try to remain upbeat, outgoing and friendly. Be as consistent as possible in terms of pick-up and drop-off times.
Toddlers may exhibit an extreme reaction when either parent is leaving. They may also throw tantrums frequently and frustrate easily. They may either refuse or demand to do everything themselves.	
PRESCHOOLERS – 3 to 5 years	
FEELINGS: Some preschoolers react with intense anger. Others are more likely to withdraw, doubting their own importance and feeling guilty for their actions. REACTIONS: Some preschoolers will be clingy and fearful, others will aggressively demand their own way. Many preschoolers will do both, changing back and forth throughout the day. They may also regress, losing some of the abilities they had gained. Bed wetting, for example, is not at all uncommon. While at play with other children, they may become aggressive or be very bossy. Transitions are likely to be difficult.	Preschoolers need consistency. They need consistent rules, expectations, and schedules. Find and develop new routines and rituals as soon as possible. If changes are needed, explain them carefully and clearly. Spend "quality time" with your preschoolers; they need to know that their parents enjoy spending time with them. Do not allow them to hurt themselves or others, but avoid excessive punishment for misbehavior. (Punishment designed to make them pay for misbehavior is not generally effective or desirable.)

YOUNG SCHOOL-AGED CHILDREN – 6 to 8 years

FEELINGS: These children react with intense feelings. They may be sad, angry, defiant, scared, confused, or lonely at any given moment. They may "take sides" but are also likely to feel loyalty conflicts strongly. They are prone to strong reconciliation fantasies.

REACTIONS: They are likely to have strong sudden outbursts of emotion. They may try to take care of their depressed or sad parents, and angrily blame the other for the divorce. At the same time, they will struggle to keep their parents focused on each other, with the hope that they will get back together. Attention to schoolwork and other parts of life outside the home may slip.

Early school-aged children need consistent and clear messages that the divorce is an adult problem and not their responsibility. They also need opportunities and encouragement to express their feelings in appropriate ways. Maintain a sensitivity and curiosity about what they may be feeling even if it is difficult to hear.

Contacting the school and letting them know what is going on is a good idea. Show them, by example, how to handle strong feelings and how you take care of yourself. Be sympathetic, but don't make promises that can't be kept.

OLDER SCHOOL-AGED CHILDREN – 9 to 12 years

FEELINGS: These children are more likely to sustain one feeling for a longer period of

This age group needs sensitive and firm guidance. They need to know you care as you set clear limits. Regulation of their behavior should not dominate your time. They may also be embarrassed and not want to share deep emotions. They may also begin to devalue themselves.

REACTIONS: They may start behaving like small adults, not allowing them to be children. They may also be rebellious and resentful. They may tend to see the divorce as one parent's fault, actively blaming or bad-mouthing the other.

relationship. Doing things together that you both enjoy can make your children feel they are worthwhile and lovable.

Maintaining and building positive relationships with other adults and their peers are also important.

You can listen carefully to your 9- to 12-year-olds without having to agree with them.

TEENAGERS – 13 to 18 years

FEELINGS: Teenagers are generally focusing on their lives in a larger world, one outside their homes. This may require masking self-doubt and other feelings. Divorce can add to the inner conflicts and doubts, thus upsetting this balance. They can become anxious or resentful, seeing their parents' lives as interfering with their "coming out" time.

REACTIONS: Some teens take on the responsibility for taking

Teens need their parents to talk honestly and openly with them. They need to feel that their opinions and desires matter. When appropriate, they should be included in making household decisions. Don't pretend to involve them if your mind is already made up, or if it is an adult decision. Teens still need firm and clear guidance.

Teens may not want to talk when you do. Think about

care of a parent. Alternately, others withdraw from family life, focusing on their peer relationships to make themselves feel at home. This can make them susceptible to trying out new, potentially dangerous activities. Their school performance may also suffer.

creating or recreating the settings where you and your teen talk most easily (for example, riding in the car, stacking wood, or ...) Try to be sensitive to their issues, while also acknowledging yours.

ADULT CHILDREN

FEELINGS: While it may seem surprising, many adult children react strongly to their parents getting divorced or involved in new relationships. They can see the parent as interfering with their happy memories and their ability to access their extended family for support. They may see one parent as being childish or self-indulgent. It may be hard for them to think of their parents as sexual beings.

REACTIONS: They may react with extreme anger. They may condemn one or both parents or even cut off contact. They may be particularly hard on new loves.

Adult children need honesty and directness. They may need to know that their parents understand how difficult the situation is for them. At the same time, they may also need to know the limits to acceptable behavior.

Acknowledge that it may take time for your adult children to become comfortable with the new situation.

Appendix B

Ideas for
Setting up a Co-Parenting Center
(Sometimes Reading a Book is Not Enough)

The Kids First Center hopes the kids' messages in this book are helpful to a broad group of parents and professionals. However, nothing can replace a personal presentation by trained and skilled facilitators. More importantly, in a co-parenting program, parents can learn from other parents through directed comments and observations. Frequently, parents do not recognize their potentially harmful behavior until they observe it in others. The Kids First programs provide a personal experience for parents which are difficult to put into mere words. This section is devoted to a brief description of how a co-parenting center benefits a community and ideas for establishing such a center, based upon the Kids First Center experiences.

Is there a need for a co-parenting center in your community?

Nationwide, too many children are caught in the emotional crossfire between separating parents. Approximately one in every two marriages ends in divorce; the separation of unmarried parents adds more children to the count. In fact, few Americans have lives untouched in some manner by divorce and separation. Yet, neither the legal system nor the mental health system (when available or affordable) is equipped to provide separating parents with practical advice and

121

information. Thus, the need is huge for a resource to fill the gap for these families.

Not only is the need huge, but the nature of the family disruption is extraordinarily complex. Separating families stumble through problems of finance, legal issues, health (both mental and physical), residential location and education, along with concerns for the children's welfare. How to balance the needs of both adults and children is always a challenge.

Who benefits from a co-parenting center in the community?

- Through the various co-parenting programs, **parents** learn to ease their children's emotional distress by accomplishing the transition in a positive way which will be maintained over the years.

- **Children** receive support in groups held for a variety of age groups so that they can share their experiences and learn positive coping skills.

- The **community** has easy access to resources and referral sources in a centralized location available to all.

- **Professionals** who work with families receive continuing education to further the goal of resolving issues of children's welfare in a productive, cooperative, non-adversarial manner, to the greatest degree possible.

What are the initial requirements?

For all the reasons stated above, your community is likely to have a population of potential consumers for services from a co-parenting center. Based on the Kids First experience, beginning a co-parenting center also requires, at least, the following:

- Committed professionals to develop and present the programs

- Supportive members of the judiciary to incorporate co-parent training as part of the separation process

- Business minded individuals willing to engage in the operations of funding, marketing and overall organizational development

Who are the professionals?

Most Kids First Programs were developed by mental health professionals and family law attorneys. This collaboration remains active because the programs are designed to be facilitated by both a mental health professional and a family law attorney, one male and one female. In addition, professionals from educational institutions, the financial world (investment, tax and valuation) and the clergy are important participants so that a co-parenting center can comprehensively serve the diverse needs of the community.

Family therapists and attorneys often meet each other over and over again in the course of their practices, with families disputing issues related to children. Frequently, the same problems are rehashed. If one insightful professional can rise above the fray to develop some common solutions to the common problems and then communicate those ideas to other professionals, productive change can follow. It only takes a few passionate professionals to lead the way to a co-parenting center.

What is the role of the judiciary?

At the very beginning of co-parenting center planning, the judiciary should be informed and consulted. The courts are the biggest referral source for co-parenting programs at the Kids First Center. States differ in their approach to co-parenting programs. In Maine, it is possible for judges and magistrates to order parents to attend such programs. The Kids First Program for Parents in High Conflict is available only by court order.

Thus, it is important for co-parenting pioneers to know the status of such programs in their own states and whether the judiciary will support their efforts. If a co-parenting center is doing its job properly, the result will not only benefit the families, but will also decrease litigation of child issues in court. The concept of a co-parenting center should be able to generate tremendous appeal to judges who usually dislike dealing with these emotional issues. Once the judiciary is convinced of the effectiveness of a co-parenting program, marketing of the programs becomes a much simpler process.

What are the business aspects of a co-parenting center?

Fundraising is essential to the viability of a co-parenting center. Frequently, the professionals who have the energy to develop and implement the programs do not also have the energy to devote to fundraising. Seldom is it possible for co-parenting programs to support themselves through fees charged for the programs. Scholarships or reduced fee agreements are required for low income parents who would be shut out of the programs if they had to pay full fees. Thus, it is very important to grow the circle of initiators to include individuals skilled in business practices.

The seed organization for the Kids First[SM] Center (originally called Resources for Divorced Families) formed a collaborative partnership with the Junior League of Portland to create a co-parenting center. The Junior League assisted with initial funding and provided essential strategic planning models to help make the Center viable.

Marketing is another essential function of a co-parenting center. Over the years, Kids First has assisted other organizations with setting up co-parenting centers. The highest rate of failure occurs when there is no strategic marketing plan in effect. If the courts take the lead in identifying participants, then additional marketing efforts can focus on maintaining a high profile in the community. The goal we work toward at the Kids First Center is to become such a common household name, that whenever parents are considering separation, the resources at the Kids First Center come to mind as the place to begin, even before filing papers with the court.

An effective co-parenting center requires an energetic and diversely skilled executive director to run the operations of the center and to communicate with a board of directors which oversees the well-being of the organization. Agencies which assist nonprofits are available in most communities and their consultation and experiences can help a co-parenting center develop the business skills required for an efficient organization.

What programs and services are provided by the Kids First℠ Center?

Thanks to years of skills, talents and knowledge contributed by an enterprising executive director and staff, along with devoted board members and volunteers, the Kids First Center, in Portland, Maine, has developed a wide variety of programs for parents, children and professionals. The Stephanie Yulita Resource and Lending Library and www.KidsFirstCenter.org provide resources and information that compliment the programs, workshops and support groups. Clients may call the Kids First Center for referrals to attorneys, therapists, mediators and various support agencies. The programs that Kids First has developed and presented include the following:

- **Kids First Program** is a four-hour Saturday morning workshop designed for parents in the beginning stages of separation to address parenting challenges and to educate parents about co-parenting skills to reduce the negative effects of separation and divorce on children. The program's focus is on the needs of children as family and marital roles undergo change. The facilitators are always a mental health professional and an attorney—one male and one female.

- **Kids First Program for Women** is designed specifically for women who have been victims/survivors of domestic violence. They learn coping and parenting skills when they are unable to co-parent with their partners because they cannot communicate with them safely.

- **Kids First Program for Step-parents** is a four hour workshop designed to help adults in step-families understand the normal difficulties experienced by each person in the new family, especially the children.

- **Kids First Program for Parents in High Conflict** is an intensive 9 week course created to meet the needs particular to parents who have been in heightened and chronic conflict. This program must be court ordered.

- **Next Step Program: Putting Conflict Aside** is a four week course in a small group setting where parents are encouraged to share their experiences and learn healthy, effective ways to parent their children. Developmental ages and stages are also discussed in depth.

- **Gay, Lesbian, Bisexual, Transgender and Questioning Families: Parenting through Separation, Transition and Divorce** is a six week course to support and educate GLBTQ parents who are leaving traditional marriages as well as same gender co-parents who are separating.

- **Separation, Divorce and Dads** helps men understand the emotional effects of their divorce and separation on their partners as well as themselves and encourages the need for them to be emotionally available to their children.

- **Separation, Divorce and Moms** covers subjects of special interest to women. The subject matter and group format are determined by the women in the group.

- **Annual Conference for Professionals** is designed to educate all professionals who work with separating and divorcing families. Nationally recognized experts are invited to present the latest research and ideas regarding the impact of separation and divorce on children. Topics have included Collaborative Divorce, High Conflict Families, the Effects of Mental Health Disorders and Domestic Violence.

- **Professional Education Series** offers workshops to discuss issues relevant to legal and clinical practices. Subjects have included:

  -- The Art of Giving Testimony in Disputed Custody Cases

  -- Best Practices when a Co-Parent Relocates to a Distant Area

- **Workshops** are held on a regular basis to address various subjects of interest to parents and professionals. Subjects have included:

  -- Divorce/Separation and the Very Young Child

  -- Impact of Divorce/Separation on Adolescents

  -- Financially Surviving Divorce

  -- Consumer's Guide to the Legal System

  -- Issues related to Domestic violence and Co-Parenting

  -- Forgiveness

This year the Kids First Center will have a positive impact on the lives of over 6,000 Maine people:

- Over 2,000 adults will attend center programs to learn how to keep their children out of the separation and divorce conflict.

- Over 200 children will attend the center's separation and divorce support groups.

- Over 250 Maine professionals will be trained through center workshops and forums about the impact of separation and divorce on children.

- Over 700 children, educators and business people will be educated about the impact of separation and divorce on Maine families.

Those at the Kids First Center highly recommend co-parenting centers as a means to fill a much needed gap in the social services available in the community. Establishing such a center can be an exciting challenge for all those who know a child caught in the middle. Best wishes!

Appendix C

What Kids Want Parents to Know
About Divorce and Separation
(In Their Own Words)

The Kids First Center conducts support groups for kids whose families are transitioning through divorce and separation. The groups give children an opportunity to talk about their feelings in a safe, comfortable setting. In addition, the children have an opportunity to develop skills and strategies to adapt to their new circumstances.

These support groups are aligned with the different developmental stages of the children:

Group I: Grades 1 – 3
Group II: Grades 4 – 6
Group III: Grades 7 – 9
Group IV: Grades 10 – 12

The following pages are taken directly from various groups. Sometimes, just a few lines speak volumes.

<u>WORRIES</u>
Group I
(Grades 1 - 3)

- Visiting parents
- Mom or Dad getting a broken heart
- Where will the pets live?
- Parents crying
- Uncomfortable questions from the new partner
- Parent kissing another adult
- Parent's feelings getting hurt if I want to live with the other parent.
- Parent paying more attention to new partner than to me
- Changing schools
- Not seeing other parent
- Going from house to house
- Missing the other parent
- New dreams about missing a parent
- Feels like I am in a circle
- Missing one parent during holidays
- Missing a pet

WHAT BUGS ME
Group II
(Grades 4 – 6)

- Going back and forth between houses

- Custody battles

- Seeing one parent less than the other

- New boyfriend or girlfriend moving in

- Cleaning

- Putting me in the middle

- Move to a new place

<u>COPING SKILLS</u>
Group II
(Grades 4 – 6)

- Change the subject

- Punch Mom's bed when mad

- Read a magazine

- Listen to music

- Ask someone to say "sorry"

- Scream

- Tire yourself out

- Challenge yourself

- Ask someone to stop

- Walk away

- Lay in bed to calm down

THE ABC's of FEELINGS
Group II
(Grades 4 – 6)
(original spelling not corrected)

A: Angry, awesome, awful, alone, annoyed

B: Bad, blamed, bored

C: Confused, confront, calm

D: Depressed, disapointed, dum, diskluded, despys

E: Emoshanul, excited

F: Fighting, fault, frustrated, frightened

G: Guilty, grostout

H: Horrible, happy, hateful, hated, heroic, hoppless, helplles

I: Invisible, ignored, irreplaceable

J: Jealous, joshed

K: Kidding, kind

L: Lazy, love, lonely, lovebly

M: Mad, meaningful

N: Nawty, nervous, nauseous

O: Outrajes

P: Private, pitiful, painful

Q: Questionable

R: Running, restless, relleved, regretful, rude, respectful

S: Sad, scared, sickning, stupid

T: Trustful, tired, tiny, terrible

U: Unsettled, ugly, unincluded, unloved

V: Vulnerable, vilent

W: Waiting

X: Xcited

Y: Yucky

Z: Zealous, zipping

FEELINGS - INSIDE and OUT
Group III
(Grades 4 – 6)

For this project, 4 hands were outlined on a chart, with descriptive feelings written on the inside and outside of the hands, depending what was showing to the world and what was going on within.

Hand 1

Inside:

- puzzled, pained, paranoid, idiotic

Outside:

- mischievous, happy, stubborn, enraged

Hand 2

Inside:

- exhausted, hurt undecided, suspicious, withdrawn, joyful

Outside:

- arrogant, regretful, disappointed, sad, pained

Hand 3

Inside:

- anxious, relieved, frustrated, confused, shocked, suspicious, happy

Outside:

- surprised, satisfied, shocked, scared, sad, happy

Hand 4

Inside:

- withdrawn, joyful, cautious

Outside:

- exhausted, disappointed, confident, sad

Support Group III

Support Group III at the Kids First Center is made up of kids in grades seven to nine, mostly 12 to 14 year olds. During a session a few years ago, one of their projects was to make a poster of "What We Want Parents to Know about Divorce and Separation."

The kids approached the poster and hand-wrote his or her advice to parents. The kids' responses are stated in their entirety in this section. Some of them may also appear throughout the book.

However, the real message of this particular poster is a small note squeezed across the top of the poster—looking like it was added after the rest of the poster was complete. It said:

We might not have said what we wrote!

The group facilitator explained these kids were afraid that if their parents saw the poster (which wouldn't happen), they might identify their kids' handwriting. Some kids wrote down a statement made by a peer to avoid being identified by writing. Though the kids were forthcoming in the group session with their advice to parents, they did not necessarily want their parents to know they had said it, or presumably let their parents know the way they felt.

Many times parents report, "Oh, the kids are doing really well." And, many times, that is probably true. However, this particular disclaimer indicates some kids are putting on a good face rather than being straightforward with parents about their feelings and wishes. Try reading the kids' advice on the next page with a picture in mind of a 12-14 year old child who is afraid to have a parent know he or she offered this advice.

Caveat: If some statements are a bit confusing, please note, the spelling has been corrected, but grammar and punctuation have not.

We might not have said what we wrote!
What We Want Parents to Know
About Divorce and Separation

1. Check with the kids before making decisions about them!

2. Don't let your anger show in front of the kids! (small devilish drawing added)

3. Don't fight over us or objects and treat us like persons!

4. Don't use tools or objects as leverage!

5. No nasty comments in front of the kids!

6. Do not put kids in the middle!!! (picture of telephone added)

7. Do not influence the kid/kids to dislike the other parent!

8. Take more time with new relationships!

9. Don't ignore the kids!

10. Don't break promises!

11. Spend time with your kids wisely!

12. Get organized!

13. Put the kids first!!